BEYOND
SHANNON
AND SEAN

By the same authors

Beyond Jennifer & Jason: An Enlightened Guide to Naming Your Baby

Beyond Charles & Diana: An Anglophile's Guide to Baby Naming

Beyond Sarah & Sam: An Enlightened Guide to Jewish Baby Naming

BEYOND SHANNON AND SEAN

AN ENLIGHTENED GUIDE
TO IRISH BABY NAMING

• • • • • • • • • • • • •

LINDA ROSENKRANTZ
& PAMELA REDMOND SATRAN

St. Martin's Press
New York

Library of Congress Cataloging-in-Publication Data

Rosenkrantz, Linda.
        Beyond Shannon & Sean : an enlightened guide to Irish baby naming
    / Linda Rosenkrantz and Pamela Redmond Satran.
            p.   cm.
        ISBN 0-312-06906-5 — 0-312-06905-7 (pbk.)
        1. Names, Personal—United States.   2. Names, Personal—Irish.
    I. Satran, Pamela Redmond.   II. Title.   III. Title: Beyond Shannon
    and Sean.
    CS2377.R68   1992
    929.4'089162—dc20   91-41546
                                                              CIP

10 9 8 7 6 5

CONTENTS

ACKNOWLEDGMENTS

The world of Irish names is mysterious not only to American parents but to many Irish parents as well. Its vocabulary is not one you can pick up by listening in playgrounds (including those in Dublin and Galway), reading newspaper birth announcements, or perusing any of dozens of naming dictionaries. Finding the hundreds of Irish names included in this book, as well as unraveling their origins and permutations over the years, involved poring over esoteric books found in specialized bookshops throughout Ireland and in London as well as in New York and Los Angeles. Sourcebooks that proved invaluable include *Irish Names* by Donnchadh Ó Corráin and Fidelma Maguire (Dublin, The Lilliput Press, 1990); *Irish Names for Children* by Patrick Woulfe (Dublin, Gill and Macmillan, 1923, revised 1974); *Pocket Guide to Irish First Names* by Ronan Coghlan (Belfast, The Appletree Press, 1985); *Book of Irish Names: First, Family & Place Names* by Ronan Coghlan, Ida Grehan, and P. W. Joyce (New York, Sterling Publishing, 1989), compiled from three books published by Appletree Press; *The First Book* and *The Second Book of Irish Myths and Legends* by Eoin Neeson (Cork and Dublin, The Mercier Press, 1990); and *Irish Folk Tales* edited by Henry Glassie (New York, Penguin Books, 1987).

Heartfelt thanks to Richard Morrissey for his help with Gaelic spellings and pronunciations in the index.

And of course, thanks to our editors, Hope Dellon and Abigail Kamen of St. Martin's Press, to our agent Molly Friedrich, and to our families, the Irish branches as well as the non.

INTRODUCTION

Your grandmother on your mother's side came from County Cork. Your great-grandfather on your father's side was from Ireland too. And your spouse is one-quarter Irish. So although—or maybe because—your last name is Smith or Taggliatella (or even if it's O'Hara), you want to give your baby an Irish first name.

The problem is: Where do you find one? Sprinkled throughout the usual naming dictionaries are names that seem to be Irish, although it's hard to tell, because while one book calls the name Bridget—a thoroughly Irish name if ever there was one—Irish, two others identify it as simply Celtic. Three books claim the name Fiona is Irish, but the fact is that it's Scottish.

And even when you do all the work yourself of culling the Irish names that are readily available and plainly identified, you're left with a pretty paltry list: heavy on the well-used Irish classics—Brian and Kevin and Kathleen—and on the Irish names trendy in recent years—Shannon and Kelly and

Sean—but nearly devoid of any names that combine Irish tradition with originality and spark.

We know, because one of us went through the same disheartening process herself when trying to find an Irish name for her first child. One of the few names that seemed to capture all the requisite qualities, Rory, was chosen for the baby. The fact that Rory was a boy's name and the baby was a girl seemed a minor hitch considering all the effort it had taken to find a good Irish name, period.

That frustration—of knowing you want a certain kind of name but having to sift through mounds of irrelevant information to find it—provided part of the inspiration for our first baby-naming book, *Beyond Jennifer & Jason: An Enlightened Guide to Naming Your Baby.* In *Beyond Jennifer & Jason,* we grouped names not alphabetically but according to parents' real-life requirements and concerns: into categories such as fashionable names, ambisexual names, biblical names, and, yes, even Irish names.

But while *Beyond Jennifer & Jason* proved to be a valuable name primer for parents interested in narrowing down the whole wide world of names, those parents whose name focus is tighter—who are interested only in Jewish names, for instance, or in Irish names for that matter—want more. Rather than a handful of Irish names within a universal name book, they want a universe of Irish names from which to choose.

That's where this book comes in. *Beyond Shannon & Sean* is by far the most comprehensive Irish name book ever published in America, and the first to offer the innovative structure that's made its parent, *Beyond Jennifer & Jason,* so popular. The array of chapters and lists you'll find here—from names fashionable among Irish-Americans to those being revived in Ireland, from names of Irish saints to names of Irish stars—can help you understand not only the full range of Irish names but find the perfect one for your child. These name lists are organized into five major sections.

From Annie to Aine, from Seamus to James: The full range of Irish first names, from those that have been popular among Irish-Americans ever since our grandmothers stepped off the boat to the names imported to Ireland that the Irish have made their own, including those names that are truly and traditionally Irish. In this section, you'll also find out why so many Irish names died out in America as well as in Ireland, and why they're being revived.

From Murphy Brown to the Hills of Donegal: Among the most fashionable names today are the Irish surname names. This section takes you from the familiar, like Murphy (Brown), Ryan (O'Neal), and Flannery (O'Connor), to the more adventurous, like Brennan, Reilly, and Gallagher. What if your last name is Gallagher? Then you may be interested to know that Charles, Conall, and Tully are all traditional names among the Gallagher clan. You'll find that kind of information if your family name is O'Connor, McArdle, or any one of dozens of others here too. Plus you'll find Irish place names that can be adopted as first names.

From King Kennedy of Munster to King Kennedy of Massachusetts: A complete list of Irish royal names—from those of medieval queens and high kings to the names favored by America's royal family, the Kennedys—for parents who want to raise a little Irish-American prince or princess.

From St. Patrick to St. Attracta: Ireland is a Catholic country, and saints' names have had a major impact on naming traditions over the years. Here you'll find the usuals, from Patrick to Bridget to Kevin, plus a veritable swarm of lesser-known saints with equally unfamiliar names, from Attracta to Keelin to Finnian to Mo Bi. If the priest flinches at the baptism, just show him this book.

From Finn MacCool to Sinead O'Connor: The Irish are perhaps best known for their stars: the mythical characters of legend and literature—from Finn MacCool to Molly Bloom—to the celebrities who've become one-person emissaries for their names, like Brendan Behan and Sinead O'Connor. Here you'll find the luminaries, both real and imaginary, and the names they have made famous.

A NOTE ABOUT PRONUNCIATION, SPELLING, AND ACCENT MARKS

Speaking of Sinead O'Connor, why is her name pronounced Shi-nayd and not Si-nee-ad? Irish spellings and pronunciations are indeed confusing, a problem we've tried to sidestep, in most cases, by emphasizing the anglicized spellings of names, which are not only more comprehensible than the Irish versions but also, in conjunction with the Irish spellings, offer a guide to pronunciation. When the Irish spelling is still relevant and used, we include that as well: GRANIA/Grainne, for example. In some cases, however, we list only the Irish version: Siobhan, in our opinion, should never be bastardized as Shavon or Shevawne, however much these spellings clarify pronunciation.

To assist you in these delicate matters, we've included a brief guide to pronunciation at the end of the book, along with notes on the pronunciation of specific names in the index. We've also included accent marks, where appropriate, only in the index, as they are often dispensed with willy-nilly in modern Irish, and seem affected and make no sense anyway to most Americans. When you decide on a name for your baby, use the accent marks at your own discretion, or peril.

Above all, don't let any of this overwhelm you. You won't actually have to try to decipher a name's pronunciation unless you decide to revive one of the more obscure names of, say, a medieval king or a seventh-century saint. With names that are well used and potentially confusing to pronounce, we've included an on-site key: We note, for instance, that Aine is pronounced *Anya* (which seems to break all of the rules of pronunciation anyway).

We can't abandon you to this book without noting that many of the Irish names here are unfamiliar: The best of them—and there are scores of good ones—could be considered appealingly fresh; there are lots of others you may simply find bizarre. Where you draw the line, and on which side of it you choose to stand, is up to you. What you'll get from this book is a full complement of Irish names, and in the end, the pleasure of knowing you've made a thoughtful and enlightened choice, whether you decide to move beyond Shannon and Sean or not.

FROM ANNIE TO AINE, FROM SEAMUS TO JAMES

Irish First Names

If you want to give your baby an Irish name, you've got a wide field from which to choose. You can decide on an Irish-American name, which usually isn't really Irish at all but simply has a green tinge. These names include the names our grandparents and great-grandparents brought with them to America—the Annies and Jameses, Mollys and Michaels—as well as "Irish" names trendy in recent years: Caitlin and Casey and Kerry and Erin.

You can also choose one of the names we think of as traditionally Irish, from the familiar Sean to the more exotic Seamus, Sinead, or Siobhan. It turns out that many of these names aren't really Irish either, but Irish forms of John, James, Jane, and Joan.

So what is an authentically Irish name? Some of these are familiar: Brian and Kevin and Bridget and Deirdre, for example. But many more, while gaining popularity in Ireland, are virtually unknown in America. Cormac, for instance, or

Conor, Grania, and Maeve. Dozens more are ripe for revival by Irish-American parents.

In this section, we offer the full range of Irish first names, from those popular in America now and in the past, to Irish forms of non-Irish names and Irish names that are truly Irish.

BALTIMORE
BRIDGETS AND
CINCINNATI SEANS

Irish Names in America

In the century from 1820 to 1920, there were 4,400,000 emigrants from Ireland to the United States, the earliest (and largest) number fleeing from rampant famine and disease. Each of these émigrés brought with him or her a name. Yet these names were not, by and large, "Irish" names. In the nineteenth century, Ireland was still in the grip of anti-Gaelic laws (which included prohibitions against the use of Gaelic names), and so the new immigrants mostly had standard "American" names: John and James, William and Thomas, Mary, Margaret, Elizabeth, and Anne. And those who had anglicized versions of favorite Irish names—Bridget or Patrick or Hugh, for instance—were often anxious to trade them in for names that sounded even less green: Bridget became Bertha or Bea, Patrick might have called himself Pete.

It was with pet forms—many of which were given to babies as proper names—that the new Irish-Americans established their own naming identity. The following names were linked closely with the old sod by the 1920s:

ANNIE	NELLY
BARNEY	PADDY
KATE	PAT
KATIE	PATSY
KITTY	PEGGY
MAGGIE	ROSIE
MICKEY	SALLY
MIKE	TESS
MOLLY	

The Irish had imported Kathleen to America in the nineteenth century, but it wasn't until the 1920s that the true impact of the Irish "een" names began to be felt. These included not only actual Irish names like Pegeen, Eileen and its variant Aileen, Maureen (a diminutive of Maire, the Irish Mary) and Noreen (a diminutive of Nora), but also Josephine, a French name that was very popular in Ireland; Doreen, an anglicization of the Irish Dorren or Doireann; and Rosaleen, the Irish pet form for Rose. Colleen—an Irish word meaning "girl" but never used in Ireland as a name—hit the New World in the 1940s, peaking in popularity in the early 1960s.

From the 1920s to the 1950s, several other Irish names trickled into the mainstream, including:

BARRY	DUANE
BRIAN	KEELEY
DARRIN/DARREN	KEVIN
DEIRDRE	MONA
DENNIS	MURIEL

MYRNA   TERRY
NEIL   TRACY
PATRICIA   TYRONE
SHEILA

Only in America

Some of the best-loved "Irish" names in America are not used in Ireland at all. If you want to give your child a truly Irish name, don't mistakenly choose one of the following:

CAITLIN: The Irish spelling for Kathleen, which, in Ireland, is pronounced *Kathleen.*
CARRICK: A name of Irish derivation (it means "rock") but never found in Ireland.
COLLEEN: Tantamount to naming your daughter "Girl."
ERIN: The Irish name for the country, not used for people.
FIONA: Although well used in Ireland, this name is a nineteenth-century Scottish invention. Similar names that are genuinely Irish are Finella and Finola.
MEGAN: A diminutive of Margaret that, while sometimes found in Ireland, is actually Welsh. The true Irish equivalent is Pegeen or Peigin.
SHANNON: In Ireland, it's strictly a river.

The sexually liberated sixties and early seventies were the perfect time for a certain kind of energetic but informal Irish name. This was when Casey and Kelly and Kerry and Stacy and Tracy took off for both sexes. Sean, Shane, Shannon, and Shauna joined the mix, as did Darcy and Donovan, Erin, Ryan, Rory, and Tara, as well as Megan. By 1975, there were nine "Irish" names among the top fifty boys' names in America:

Name	Rank
BRIAN	4
KEVIN	19
SEAN	20
RYAN	23
PATRICK	38
SHANE	39
JUSTIN	45
DONALD	48
DENNIS	50

For girls, we saw the following names in the top fifty a few years earlier:

Name	Rank
TRACY	5
KELLY	6
STACEY	18
SHANNON	23
PATRICIA	35

While some of these "Irish" names have fallen from favor over the past decade, others continue to climb in popularity.

As of this writing, Justin, a name scarcely used outside Ireland in the first half of the twentieth century, is number eight on the American hit parade, and Ryan is number thirteen. For girls, the Irishy Megan is number eight.

Other trends are beginning to emerge. One is that more truly Irish names, as opposed to those that simply have an Irish flavor, are growing in favor. Brendan, for example, the name of a sixth-century Irish saint, is gaining in popularity, as is the trendy Caitlin (the Irish spelling of Kathleen), and Liam, an Irish pet form of William. The following Irish names, some attached to the new generation of international Irish rock and movie stars, are also in the forefront of fashion:

G I R L S

BRIANA	SIOBHAN (but not the
MAEVE	phoneticized Sha-
MAIRE	vonne or Shevon)
SINEAD	

B O Y S

AIDAN	KILLIAN
CON(N)OR	LAUGHLIN
DECLAN	LORCAN
DERMOT	MALACHY
DESMOND	PADRAIG
EAMON	ROHAN
FINNIAN	SEAMUS
HUGH	

Some names that have been traditionally used only for boys in Ireland have become new ambisexual choices in America. These names include:

DARRIN/DARREN	TIARNAN/TIERNAN
KIERAN	TIERNEY
RORY	

Murphy Brown has helped kick off the popularity of another large group of Irish names that can be used for both boys and girls, the Irish surname names. For a comprehensive list of these, see pages 52–54.

The other major trend? As trends do, this one comes full circle, back to the names (or more often, the nicknames) of our Irish grandmas and grandpas who originally emigrated to the United States, bringing their names with them. This picks up on a general enthusiasm for Grandma and Grandpa names that we noted in *Beyond Jennifer & Jason:* the Maxes and Mollys, Harrys and Hannahs who are crowding the nurseries and playgrounds at the moment. The Grandma and Grandpa names being revived by today's Irish-American parents include:

G I R L S

ANNIE	KATE
BRIDGET	KAY
FANNY	KITTY
FRANNIE	LIZZIE
JENNY	MAGGIE
JOSIE	MAMIE

MAY   PATSY
MINNIE   PEGGY
MOLLY   ROSIE
NELL/NELLY   TESS
NORA   TILLIE

B O Y S

CHARLIE   MAC
FRANK (for Francis X.)   MICKEY
JACK   NED
JOE   PAT/PATRICK
JOHNNY   TOM

TRADITIONAL IRISH NAMES

There are hundreds of names that can be considered truly Irish, springing from Ireland's own culture and language. Most of these names were anglicized during Britain's three-hundred-year occupation of Ireland—with many old names lost forever in the process—but Irish independence in the 1920s spurred the rediscovery of a host of traditional Irish names. In 1923, an Irish priest, Patrick Woulfe, wrote *Irish Names for Children,* a book that made these native names as well as the Irish forms of popular imports (Padraig for Patrick, for example) well known and well accepted once again.

Purists may argue that the Irish spellings of these names should always be used; however, we have emphasized the anglicized spelling in most cases, following the lead of the majority of Irish parents who choose Irish names for their children. Because so many of the names are foreign in themselves—and the Irish spellings so often cumbersome and baffling to pronounce—we feel the anglicized spelling is usually the only one that makes sense for Irish-American parents. In some cases, however, when the Irish spelling is the only one (or the predominant one) used, or when the name's "translation" has been hopelessly corrupted, we've given the Irish spelling. The girl's name Aoife—a beautiful name that's wildly popular among modern Irish parents—is a case in point. While Aoife is pronounced and can be anglicized as Eva, it actually has no relation to that name and is better left in its well-used original form.

What follows are purely Irish names that are still used in modern times. For more unusual Irish names (although many listed here are pretty unusual) that may have become obsolete, see the lists of Irish queens and kings, legendary figures, and saints. For the Irish versions of non-Irish names, consult the translation charts on pages 25–29, or see the section, "More Irish Than the Irish," which follows. Note: The first, capitalized version of each name is the preferred one. When the second version is also capitalized, it's an equally acceptable alternate spelling of the name.

G I R L S

AIDAN	ALVA/Almha
AIDEEN	ANA
AILEEN	AOIFE/Eva
AINE (pronounced	AURNIA
Anya)	BAINE
AISLING/Aislinn	BANBHA
ALANA/ALANNAH	BARRAN
ALASTRINA/	BEIBHINN (pronounced
Alistriona	*Bevin*)
ALMA	BETHA

BIDELIA
BLANAID
BLINNE/Blanche
BRIDGET/Brid (the
 Old Irish form is BRI-
 GIT)
CAOILINN (pro-
 nounced *Kelin*)
CEARA (pronounced
 Cara or *Kyra*)
CLODAGH
CLORA/Clothra
COCHRANN
COLUMBA/Colma
CONNA
CONNAL
CORCAIR
DAIRINE
DANA
DARERCA
DAROVA/
 Dar Oma
DAVNIT/
 Damhnait
DEALLA
DECLA
DEIRDRE
DERINN/Dairinn
DERVAL/Dearbhail
DERVILA/Deirbhile
DERVOGILLA/
 Dearbhorgaill
DORREN/Doireann

DUNLA/Dunlaith
DUVESSA/Duibheasa
DYMPHNA/Damhnait
EAVAN/Aoibhinn
EILIS(E)
EITHNE (rhymes with
 henna)
ELAN
ELVA/Ailbhe
EMER/Eimhear (pro-
 nounced *ever*)
ENAT/Aodhnait
ETAIN (pronounced
 Eden)
ETHNA
EVEGREN/Aoibhgreine
EVLIN/Eibhleann
FAINCHE
FARVILA/Forlaith
FENNORE/Fionnuir
FIDELMA
FINN
FINOLA/Fionnuala
FLANN
FLANNAIT
GOBNAIT
GORMLAITH/Gormley
GRANIA/Grainne
HODIERNA
ISEULT
ITA
KEAVY/Caoimhe
KEENAT/Ciannait

KELLY/Ceallach
LASRINA/Lasairiona
MACHA
MAEVE/Meadhbh
MAILLE
MAILSE
MAIRONA
MAITI (pronounced
  Matty)
MARGO
MEALLA
MEEDA
MOINA
MOIRA
MONA(T)
MOR
MOREEN/
  Moirin
MORNA
MORRIN
MUGAIN
MUIREANN (pro-
  nounced *Myron*)
MYRNA/
  Muirne
NARVLA/Narbhla
NESS(A)

NIAMH (Niav is the
  phonetic anglicized
  spelling, not often
  used in Ireland)
NUALA
ORLA
ORNA(T)
PHIALA
RENNY
RIONA
RONAIT
SAMHAOIR
SAORLA
SARAID
SCOTA
SINE/Sheena
SIVE
SLANY/Slaine
SORCHA
TAILLTE (pronounced
  Talty)
TALULLA/Tuilelaith
TARA/Teamhair
TEFFIA/Teafa
TUATHLA (pro-
  nounced *Tuala*)
UNA

B O Y S

AENGUS
AICHLINN
AIDAN/Aodhan
AILILL
ALAN
ANLON
ARDAL
ART
BANAN
BARDAN
BARHAN/Bearchan
BARRY/Bairre
BECCAN
BRAN
BRANDUFF/Brandubh
BRAZIL
BRIAN
BRION
BROGAN
BRONE
CADHLA
CAFFAR/Cathbharr
CAHIR/Cathair
CAIRBRE
CALLAGHAN
CALVAGH
CANICE/Coinneach
CANOC
CARROLL/Cearbhall
CATHAL

CELSUS
CIAN/Kean
COLE/Comhghall
COLLA
COLM
COLMAN
COLMCILLE
COLUMBA
CONAIRE
CONALL/CONNELL
CONAN
CONLEY
CONN
CON(N)OR
CORBAN
CORC
CORMAC
COWAN
DALLAN
DAMAN
DARRAGH
DARREN
DAVIN/Daimhin
DECLAN
DERMOT/Diarmaid
DONAGH/Donnchadh
DONAL
DONEGAN
DONLEAVY
DONOVAN

DOUGAL/Dubhghall
DUALD
DUFFY
EACHANN
EGAN/Aodhgan
ENDA
ENOS
EOGHAN (pronounced
Owen)
ERNAN
EVENY/Aibhne
FACHTNA
FARRELL/Fearghal
FELIM(ID)
FERGAL
FERGUS/Fearghus
FIACH
FIACHRA
FINBAR
FINEEN/Finin
FIN(N)IAN
FINN
FINNEGAN
FINTAN
FLANAGAN
FLANN
GAEL
GALVIN
GARVIN
GILPATRICK
GILLEECE/Giolla Iosa
GLAISNE
GLAS

GORMAN
GRIFFIN/Criofan
GUAIRE
HEBER/Eibhear
HEWNEY/Uaithne
HUGH/Aodh
JARLATH/Iarlaith
KEAN/Cian (pro-
nounced Cane)
KEDAGH/Ceadach
KELLY/Cellach
KENNEDY/Cinneide
KENNELLY/Cionnaola
KERILL/Caireall
KEVAN
KEVIN
KIERAN/Ciaran
KILIAN/Cillin
KINSELLA/Cinnsealach
LEARY/Laoghaire
LENNAN
LOCHLAINN
LOMAN
LORAN/Luaran
LORCAN
LUCAN
LYNAGH/Laighneach
LYSAGH/Looiseach
MACARTAN
MACCON
MAHON
MALACHY (pro-
nounced Malakey)

MANNIX/Mainchin
MANY/Maine
MARCAN
MEL
MIACH
MOLLOY
MULRONEY
MURRAY/Muirioch
MURROUGH/
    Murchadh
MURTAGH/
    Muircheartach
NATHY/Naithi
NESSAN
NEVAN
NIADH
NIALL (pronounced
    Neil)
NIALLAN
ORAN

OSCAR
OSSIAN/Oisin
QUINLAN/Caoinlean
QUINTON/Cumhai
REILLY
RIORDAN
RONAN
RORY/Ruairi
ROSS
ROWAN
RYAN/Rian
SCANLON
SEANAN
SHEEDY/Sioda
TADHG (rhymes with
    league)
TIARNAN
TIERNEY/Tiarnach
TULLY/Tuathal
TURLOUGH/Tarlach

MORE IRISH THAN
THE IRISH

Several of those names that we think of as most Irish are not really Irish at all but imports introduced by the Catholic Church or by Norman and English invaders. But Ireland, once thought to be the end of the world and therefore the last stop for many European adventurers, has long absorbed the influences of other cultures. Indeed, it is said in Ireland that outsiders often become "more Irish than the Irish," and these Irishized forms of foreign names—among the best known and most popular not only in America but in Ireland itself—prove the point. While their origins may be Latin, French, or Hebrew, their souls are shamrock green:

G I R L S

CAITLIN/Kathleen
(pronounced *Kath-leen*)
CATRIONA/Caitriona
EILEEN/Eibhlin
FIONA (Scottish form
of Fionnuala)
MAIRE (Irish form of
Mary; pronounced
Marie)
MAIREAD (pro-
nounced *May Reed*)

MAUREEN/Mairin
NORA(H)
NOREEN/Noirin
PATRICIA
ROSALEEN/Roisin
ROSE/Rois
SHEILA/Sile
SINEAD
SIOBHAN

B O Y S

BRENDAN
COLIN
EOIN (pronounced
Owen)
GARRETT/Gearoid
LIAM

OWEN
PATRICK/Padraig
REDMOND/Reamonn
SEAMUS
SEAN

MOST POPULAR
IRISH NAMES

Aine or Baine? Donal or Donovan? It's difficult to get any real sense of how reasonable—or strange—a name is when you see it totally out of context; that is, when you're in New Jersey but the name has been heretofore used only in Dublin. Of course, the best guide to whether a name is right for you is your own taste and sensibility. However, here's a guide to what the one-third or so of contemporary Irish parents who choose Irish names for their children consider to be the "best" Irish names. For other popular names in Ireland, see "More Irish Than the Irish."

G I R L S

AINE	CEARA
AISLING/Aislinn	DEIRDRE
AOIFE	DERVAL/Dearbhail

EAVAN
EILIS(E)
EITHNE
EMER
ETAIN
FINOLA
GORMLAITH

GRANIA/Grainne
MAEVE
NIAMH
ORLA
SAORLA
SORCHA
UNA

B O Y S

AENGUS
AIDAN
BRIAN
COLMAN
CONALL/CONNELL
CON(N)OR
CORMAC
DECLAN
DERMOT/Diarmaid
DONAGH
DONAL

FINBAR
FINN
FINTAN
HUGH
KEVIN
KIERAN
LORCAN
MALACHY
NIALL
RONAN
RORY

DOES BRIAN EQUAL BARNEY?

Irish Names and Their English Translations

For nearly three hundred years, when all of Ireland was under British rule, native Irish names were subverted in favor of their English "equivalents"—many of which were not so equivalent. It's difficult to see, from this perspective, why Brian should become Barney, how Una translates to Agnes, or why anyone would choose these English forms over the Irish originals unless someone was holding a gun to his head. However, that's exactly what happened in Ireland during the years of British domination: Gaelic names were forbidden along with the Gaelic language, and all the little girls who might have been Aine were by force named Anne.

Since the 1920s, however, when most of Ireland finally became independent, Irish parents have largely pulled Maeve back from the clutches of Madge and Marjorie; chosen Aisling over Esther; favored Aengus rather than Aeneas, the odious Enos, or even the perfectly respectable but totally unrelated Nicholas. As is evident from this list, the Irish forms have in most cases become more predominant than their outmoded English stand-ins.

Some names were improved by translation, however, and it is these that live on in their "new" forms. Malachy, for instance, is infinitely more melodious and accessible than Maolmhaodhog, and Hugh more comprehensible than Aodh.

Those of you who wish to name a child after an Irish grandmother or great-grandfather—only to be stumped to find his or her name was the distinctly un-Irish Grace or

---

The Owen Question

The name Owen (to use its phonetic and most familiar form) illustrates how confusing it can be to untangle the threads of genuine Irish names versus their anglicized translations versus imports made Irish.

Eoghan, pronounced *Owen,* is an ancient and once widely used Irish name that was eventually anglicized as Eugene (a name with Greek origins) and Owen, a Welsh name. John, obviously an import, was Irishized to Sean and Eoin, which is also pronounced *Owen.*

Today, Eoghan the original, Owen its anglicization, and Eoin the Irishization of John are generally thought of as different spellings of the same name. While by pronunciation all three may be authentically Irish, the version considered the most solidly Irish is ironically the one with the shakiest connection to the name's Irish origins: Eoin.

Laurence—may want to use this list to affect a reverse translation. If this is your intention, consult also the list of Irishizations on pages 30–33: Grandma Maggie may become baby Mairead and Grandpa Bill may live on as little Liam.

G I R L S

Irish	Anglo
AINE	Anna
	Anne
	Hannah
AOIFE	Eva
AISLING/AISLINN . . .	Alice
	Esther
ALMHA	Alva
BEIBHINN	Bevin
	Vivian
BLINNE	Blanche
DOIREANN	Dolly
	Doreen
	Dorothy
EITHNE	Annie
ELVA	Olive
FAINCHE	Fanny
FINOLA/	
FIONNUALA	Flora
	Penelope
FLANN	Florence
GOBNAIT	Abigail
	Deborah
GORMLAITH	Barbara
GRANIA/GRAINNE . .	Grace
LUIGHSEACH	Lucy

MAEVE	Mabel
	Madge
	Marjorie
	Maude
MAILLE	Molly
MOIRNE	Maria
	Maud
MOR	Agnes
	Martha
	Mary
MUADHNAIT	Mona
MUIREANN	Marion
RIONA	Regina
SARAID	Sarah
SIVE	Sabia
	Sally
	Sarah
	Sophia
SORCHA	Sally
	Sarah
TAILLTE	Taltena
UNA	Agnes
	Juno
	Unity
	Winifred

B O Y S

Irish	Anglo
AENGUS	AENEAS
	EENIS/Enos
	NICHOLAS
AIBHNE	Aveny
AILBHE	Albert
	Bertie

AILILL	Elias
	Irial
AINEISLIS	Standish
	Stanislaus
ANAMCHA	Ambrose
AODH	Hugh
AODHAN	Aidan
ARTGAL	Arnold
BAIRRE	Barry
BEIRCHEART	Benjamin
	Bernard
BRIAN	Barnaby
	Barney
	Bernard
CAINNEACH	Canice
	Kenny
CALBHACH	Charles
CATHAL	Charles
CATHAOIR	Charles
CEARBHALL	Charles
CONCHOBHAR	Cornelius
CONN	Constantine
CORMAC	Charles
CU COIGRICHE	Peregrine
CUMHAI	Cooey
	Hughey
	Quinton
DIARMAID	Dermot
	Derry
	Jeremiah
DONAL	Daniel
DONNCHADH	Denis
	Dionysius
	Donagh
DUALTACH	Dudley
DUNLANG	Dowling
	Dudley

EARNAN	Ernest
EIBHEAR	Harry
	Heber
	Ivor
EIGNEACHAN	Ignatius
EIMHIN	Evan
EOGHAN	Eugene
	Owen
EOLANN	Olan
EIREAMHON	Irwin
FACHTNA	Fantasius
	Festus
FEARADHACH	Ferdinand
	Fergus
	Frederick
FIACHA	Festus
FININ	Florence
	Florry
FLANN	Florence
GIOLLA CHRIOST . .	Christian
GIOLLA NA NAOMH	Nehemias
GLAISNE	James
LACHTNA	Lucius
LAISREN	Lazarus
LAOISEACH	Lewis/Louis
	Lucius
LOCHLAINN	Laurence
LORCAN	Laurence
LUCHAIDH	Aloysius
	Lewis/Louis
MAELECHLAINN	Malachy
MAODHOG	Aidan (Protestants)
	Moses (Catholics)
MAOLMHAODHOG .	Malachy
MAOL MHORDHA . .	Myles
MAOL MHUIRE	Milo
	Murray
	Myles

MUIRCHEARTACH .	Maurice
	Mortimer
	Murtaugh
MUIRIOCH	Murray
MUIRIOS	Maurice
MURCHADH	Morgan
	Murrough
NAOISE	Noah
NIALL	Nicholas
	Nigellus
RUAIRI/RORY	Richard
	Roderick
	Roger
SEANAN	Senan
	Simon
SUIBHNE	Simon
TADHG	Ted
	Timothy
TARLACH	Charles
	Terry/Terence
	Turlough
TOMALTACH	Thomas
	Timothy
UAITHNE	Anthony
	Hewney
	Owney

IRISHIZATIONS

In the fifth, sixth, and seventh centuries, the priests brought news of saints and European pilgrimages to Ireland. Then in the eighth century the Norse invaded, followed by the Anglo-Normans in the twelfth century. Oliver Cromwell claimed Ireland for Britain in the seventeenth century. What they all left behind, when the Republic of Ireland was once again independent in the 1920s, were their names.

Of course, many non-Irish names became popular, and remain so to this day, in their unadulterated forms. But many others were Irishized: translated into Gaelic and popularized as "Irish" names in their own right. Here are the names that invaded Ireland and the Irish names they became:

GIRLS

Non-Irish Name	"Irish" Version
Abigail	ABAIGEAL
Agatha	AGATA
Agnes	AIGNEIS
Alexandra	ALASTRIONA
Alice	AILIS
Amelia	AIMILIONA

Anastasia	ANNSTAS
Annabel(la)	ANNABLA
	NABLA
Barbara	BAIRBRE
Carina	CAIREANN
Catherine	CAITRIONA
Cecilia	SILE/SHEILA
Charlotte	SEARLAIT
Christine	CRISTIN
Christina	CRISTIONA
Eleanor	AILIONORA
Elizabeth	EILIS
Emily	EIMILE
Esther	EISTIR
Frances	PROINNSEAS
Honor(a)	NORA(H)
	NOREEN/NOIRIN
	ONORA
Isabel	ISIBEAL
	SIBEAL
Jane	SINEAD
Jean(ne)	SINE/SHEENA
Joan	SIOBHAN
Josephine	SEOSAIMHIN
Marcella	MAIRSIL
Margaret	MAIREAD
Mary	MAIRE
Meg	PEIG
Patricia	PADRAIGIN
Rose	ROIS
Susan	SUSANNA
Teresa	TREASA

B O Y S

Non-Irish Name	"Irish" Version
Adam	ADHAMH
Alexander	ALASTAR
Arthur	ARTUR
Brendanus	BRENDAN
Colin	COILIN
David	DAIBHEAD
	DAIBHI
Edmund	EAMONN
Felix	FELIC
Francis	PROINNSIAS
Geoffrey	SHEARY
	SHERON
Gerald	GEAROID
Henry	ANRAOI
	ENRI
John	EOIN
	SEAN
Joseph	SEOSAMH
Luke	LUCAS
Magnus	MANUS
Martin	MAIRTIN
Matthew	MAITIU
	MATHA
Michael	MICHEAL
Nicholas	NICOL
	NIOCLAS
Noah	NOE
Olaf	AULIFFE
Patrick	PADRAIG
Paul	POL
Peter	PEADAR
Philip	PILIB
Piers	PIARAS

Raymond	REAMONN
	REDMOND
Reginald	RAGHNALL
Richard	RIOCARD
Solomon	SOLAMH
Stephen	STIOFAN
Thomas	TOMAS
William	LIAM
	UILLIAM

IRELAND'S NATIONAL NAME

Patrick, the national name of Ireland, is not Irish at all but a derivation of the Latin name Patricius. But when St. Patrick landed in Ireland in the fifth century, he convinced the Irish to embrace his name as well as his religion. So revered was St. Patrick that his name, like the Virgin Mary's, was not used by mere mortals until the seventeenth century. Before that time, people used forms such as Gilla Patraic (the equivalent of the modern Gilpatrick, meaning servant of St. Patrick) or Mael Patraic, which means devotee of St. Patrick.

But like Mary, Patrick became a wildly popular name once it started being used. It has spawned an overwhelming number of variations both in English and Irish Gaelic. The most common Irish form—Padraig, pronounced *Pahrig*—is used more often in Ireland today than the anglicized Patrick. However, Patrick in any form has in recent years been slipping in the Irish popularity polls, although it is newly on the upswing in both England and America.

Patricia and the Irish Padraigin are female variations of the name. The male variants and diminutives of Patrick include:

FITZPATRICK
GILPATRICK
MAELPATRICK
PA
PADDY
PADHRA
PADHRAIC
PADRAIC
PADRAIG
PAID
PAIDI

PAIDIN
PAITI
PARAIC
PARRA
PAT
PATRAIC
PATRIC
PATSY
PAXTON
PEYTON

A MARY BY ANY OTHER NAME

In Ireland as in the rest of the Christian world, Mary was thought to be too sacred a name for mortal use until the seventeenth century. But once people started using it, they kept using it . . . a lot. In fact, until the 1950s, Mary and its variations was almost without fail the most popular name for girls in all of the Christian countries, including both Ireland and the United States.

If "new" names like Linda and Susan supplanted Mary as the favorite choices of American parents from the 1950s onward, Irish Catholics clung to the name—in one form or another—because it conferred instant holiness on any name it was paired with. Irish-Americans used it, or more often Marie, liberally as a middle name: Lynn Marie, Donna Marie, Kelly Marie, you get the idea. Some used Mary as a "silent" first name: Robert and Ethel Kennedy, for instance, named one daughter Mary Kerry and another Mary Courtney but called the girls by their "heathen" middle names.

Other Irish-American parents played it somewhat

straighter, calling their daughters Mary but adding a middle name; anything from the sanctified Mary Ann or Mary Margaret to the "wild" (but still blessed) Mary Jo or Mary Sue, and from the upscale Mary Davis or Mary Stuart to the cute Mary Pride and Mary Joy.

Of course, Mary variations are also popular among Irish-American parents: Mara, Maura, Maureen, Maria, Molly.

While Mary in its unadorned state, like Patrick, is now falling from grace in Ireland, it is estimated that one out of four Irish females still bears the name. Besides its religious significance, of obvious appeal to the large Catholic population, the popularity of Mary in Ireland also derives from its use as an anglicization for the native (and unrelated) name Mor, overwhelmingly the most popular Irish name throughout the Middle Ages. The two names and their diminutives have become so intertwined that they're now virtually indistinguishable.

The true Irish version of Mary, however, is Maire, which is usually pronounced *Marie*. Marie and Maria have also recently increased in popularity (along with other continental imports), joining the bewildering list of Mary equivalents used in Ireland. These variations of the name include:

CARMEL	MAMIE
DOLORES	MARIA
MAILLE	MARIAN/MARION
MAILSE	MARIE
MAILTI	MAURA
MAIRE	MAUREEN
MAIRIN	MAY
MAIRONA	MEARS
MALLAIDH	MOIRA

MOLL
MOLLY
MOR
MOREEN/Moirin

MORRIN
MOYRA
MUIREANN
POLLY

FROM MURPHY BROWN TO THE HILLS OF DONEGAL

Irish Family Names and Place Names

Did you know that if your last name is O'Rourke, you can count Tiarnan and Farrell as family names? Or, if O'Rourke is your maiden name, have you considered giving your child Rourke as a first name? Or have you thought about choosing an Irish place name—Carra or Galway or even Donegal—for your child?

This section provides a guide to which first names are traditional in which families, plus a selection of Irish surnames and place names that can work as first names.

IRISH FAMILY NAMES

Many Irish families have traditionally used the same first names for generations. Some of these family names have died out in recent years; others were lost by branches of the families that emigrated to America. But all of them were used consistently enough for long enough to be considered true family names.

Unfortunately, most of the names on record are male ones. Ireland is a patriarchal society, and the males in a family were often noted while the females were ignored, at least in writing. Also, names tend to be passed down through the male line in Ireland, while girls are less often named after mothers or grandmothers.

Still, this list includes a wide number of families and, in some cases, a wide number of names within each family. The obvious way to use this information is to look for the surnames relevant to your family—your last name, for instance, as well as your grandmother's maiden name—and find the first names that are associated with them. Remember that

Why Gofraidh Isn't on This List

Gofraidh, pronounced *guffry* and sometimes anglicized to Gotty, Gorry, or Geoffrey, was once a popular name, particularly among the O'Kane family. But in 1880 one Gofraidh MacCionnaith left a deathbed curse on any of his descendants who would revive the name.

Oh, well. We didn't like it that much anyway.

families often dropped the prefixes Mac, Mc, and O over time: so if your last name is Kelly, then you can consider Grania and Malachy, two names here attributed to the O'Kelly clan, your family names.

We do need to note that many of these family names are, as family names tend to be, weird. Unhappy may be the father whose heart soars to spot his surname O'Madden on the list, only to sink when he finds out his family names are Ambrose, Breasal, and Coganus. We think, however, that some families will be cheered by their options. The MacCanns get Loughlin, Malachy, Quinton, Redmond, and Rory, for example; and among the O'Briens' selections are Connor, Kennedy, and Lucius for boys, Finola and the interesting Caoimhinn (pronounced *Kevin*) for girls. And if you can't live with one of your designated names as a first name, you may want to consider using it for your child's middle name.

One more note: When more than one form of a name is given here, the first, capitalized version is the one most generally and recently used by the family. Notice that some Irish names were anglicized differently by different families: The O'Haras translate Cian as Kean, for example, while the O'Mahoneys turn it into the biblical Cain.

Here are some Irish families and their traditional names:

G I R L S

Family	Name
Losse	WITHYPOLL
Lowther	JANA
MacDermott	DERVAL/DERBAIL
	FINOLA/FIONNUALA
	LASRINA/Lasairiona
MacDonagh	LASRINA/Lasairiona
MacNamara	SLAINE
MacNamee	GRANIA/Grainne
McCourt	AISLINN
O'Beirne	LASRINA/Lasairiona
O'Brien	CAOIMHINN (pronounced *Kevin*)
	FINOLA/Fionnuala
	SLAINE
O'Connor	ETAIN
	FINOLA/Fionnuala
O'Duffy	GRANIA/Grainne
O'Flannagan	ETAIN
O'Gormley	GRANIA/Grainne
O'Hanley	LASRINA/Lasairiona
O'Hara	ETAIN
O'Kane	AISLINN
	ROIS (pronounced *Rose*)
O'Kelly	GRANIA/Grainne
O'Murray	ROIS (pronounced *Rose*)
Toler-Aylward	ZINNA
Wallis	EDITHA

B O Y S

Family	Name
Barrett	TOIMILIN
Barry	DOWLE
Bradley	EVENY/AIBHNE
	MURTAGH/MUIRCHEARTACH
Brady	MAZIERE
Brody	EVENY/Aibhne
Burke	FESTUS/Fiacha
	UILLEAG
	UILLIAM (pronounced *William*)
Campbell	COLIN
Clibborn	ABRAM
Dalton	PHILPOG
Fitzgerald	GARRET
Foley	ENOS
Glenny	ISAAC
Joyce	GILL
Kavanagh	ART
	DOWLING/Dunlang
	GRIFFIN/Criofan
	MORGAN/Murchadh
MacAlister	AENEUS/Oengus
MacArdle	MALACHY
	REDMOND/Reamonn
MacBrannon	CONN
	MANY/Maine
MacBreen	MANY/Maine
MacBrennan	AVERKAGH
MacCabe	AIRDGAL
MacCann	LOCHLAINN
	MALACHY
	QUINTON/Comhai
	REDMOND/Reamonn
	RORY/Ruaidri
MacCarten	AUGHOLY/EUGENIUS/Echmhilidh

MacCarthy	CALLAGHAN/Ceallachan
	DERMOT/Diarmaid
	FLORENCE/Finin
	JUSTIN
MacCawell	QUINTON/Cumhai
MacClancy	BOETIUS
MacCloskey	MANUS
	QUINTON/Cumhai
MacCormack	AENEUS/Oengus
MacCoughlin	ROSS
MacDermott	CHRISTIAN/Giolla Crhiost
	MYLES/Maolruanai
MacDonagh	BRIAN
MacDonnell	AENEAS/Oengus
	ALASTAR
	COLLA
	FREDERICK/Fearachach
	RANDAL
	RORY/Ruaidri
	SORLEY
MacDowell	ALASTAR
MacEgan	BEOLAGH
	LUKE
	NEHEMIAS/Giolla na Naomh
MacElligot	ELIAS/Uilleag
MacFaden	MANUS
MacGillespie	CHARLES/Tarlach
MacGovern	BRIAN
	TIARNAN
MacKenna	LOCHLAINN
MacKiernan	ART
	DURKAN/Duarcan
	TIARNAN
Macken	REDMOND/Reamonn
MacLoughlin	MURTAGH/Muircheartach
	OSCAR

MacMahon	AIRDGAL
	BRIAN
	CULLO/Cu Ula
	GLAISNE
	IRIAL
	QUINTON/Cumhai
	ROSS
MacMasterson	DURKAN/Duarcan
MacMurrough	ART
MacNamara	CUVEA/Cumhea
	MACCON
	SHEEDY
MacNamee	FARRELL
	LOCHLAINN
	SOLOMON/Solam
MacNicholl	MANUS
MacSweeney	CHARLES/Tarlach
	DOUGAL/Dubhghall
	EOGAN (pronounced *Owen*)
	IRWIN/Eireamhon
Magawley	AWLEY
Magennis	AUGHOLY/EUGENIUS/Echmhilidh
	EIBHIR
	GLAISNE
Maguire	CONSTANTINE/Cu Chonnacht
	DONN
	OSCAR
	PILIB
	ROSS
Malone	LOCHLAINN
McGinley	RORY/Ruaidri
McRory	AIRDIN
Mulloy	RORY/Ruaidri
Nugent	BALTHASAR
O'Boyle	DOUGAL/Dubhghall
	FARRELL

O'Breslin	CHARLES/Tarlach
O'Brien	ANLON/Anluan
	ANVIRRE/Ainmire
	BRAN
	CONNOR/Conchobar
	DERMOT/Diarmaid
	DONAGH/Donnchadh
	KENNEDY
	LUCIUS/Laoiseach
	MURROUGH/Murchadh
	TERENCE/Tarlach
O'Brody	DAIRE
O'Byrne	FIACHA
	GARRETT-MICHAEL
	UGHAIRE (pronounced *Uri*)
O'Carroll	MULRONEY/Maolruanai
O'Clerkin	FARRELL
O'Clery	CONAIRE
	LEWIS/Lugaid
	TULLY/Tuathal
O'Connell	MAURICE/Muirgheas
	MORGAN/Murchadh
O'Connelly	AIRDGAL
O'Connor	ART
	BRIAN
	CHARLES/Calbhach
	CONNOR/Conchobar
	DERMOT/Diarmaid
	FAILGHE
	MACBETH/MacBeatha
	OSCAR
	OWEN/Eogan
	RODERICK/Ruaidri
	THOMAS/Tomaltach
O'Daly	BOWES/Baolach
O'Dempsey	FINN
O'Dempster	FAILGHE

O'Doherty . . . . CONALL
                              RORY/Ruaidri
                              TOIMILIN
O'Donnell . . . . AINEISLIS
                              CAFFAR/Cathbharr
                              CONALL
                              CONN
                              EOGAN (pronounced *Owen*)
                              HUGH/Aodh
                              MANUS
                              NECHTAN
                              NEILL/Niall
                              RORY/Ruaidri
O'Donoghue . . . . AULIFFE/Amhlaoibh
                              GEOFFREY/Seafra
O'Donovan . . . . AINEISLIS
                              MORGAN/Murchadh
O'Dowd . . . . TOMHAS
O'Driscoll . . . . FINN
                              FOTHAD
                              MACCON
O'Dunne . . . . FAILGHE
O'Fallon . . . . COGANUS/Cofach
O'Falvey . . . . DONNCUAN
O'Farrell . . . . CANOC/Conmhac
                              FESTUS/Fachtna
                              KEDAGH/Ceadach
                              IRIAL
                              ROSS
O'Flaherty . . . . MAONACH
O'Flanagan . . . . MALACHY
O'Flynn . . . . CULLO/Cu Ula
                              QUINTON/Cumhai
O'Gallagher . . . . CHARLES/Tarlach
                              CONALL
                              TULLY/Tuathal
O'Gormley . . . . SORLEY

O'Grady .... STANDISH
O'Halloran .... EREVAN/Eireamhon
O'Hanlon .... REDMOND/Reamonn
O'Hanly .... BARRY/Berach
O'Hara .... DURKAN/Duarcan
                          IRRILL/OLIVER/Ailill
                          KEAN/Cian
O'Herlihy .... CALLAGHAN/Ceallachan
O'Higgins .... TULLY/Tuathal
O'Hogan .... CRONEY
O'Kane .... ECHLIN
                          EVENY/Aibhne
                          JARMY
                          MANUS
                          QUINTON/Cumhai
O'Keeffe .... CORC
                          FINGUINE
                          GORMAN
O'Kelly .... BREASAL
                          BRINE
                          FERADACH
                          FESTUS/Fiacha
                          LAURENCE/Lochlainn
                          MALACHY
                          MANY/Maine
                          NEILL/Niall
                          UILLIAM (pronounced *William*)
O'Kennedy .... DONN
O'Lafferty .... EIBHIR
O'Lohan .... AMHRA (pronounced *Avra*)
O'Loughlin .... IRIAL
O'Madden .... AMBROSE/Anamcha
                          BREASAL
                          COGANUS/Cofach
O'Mahoney .... CAIN/Cian
                          FININ
                          MOLLOY/Maol Mhuire
O'Mara .... ELAN

O'Meehan	LAZARUS/Molaisse
O'Molloy	GREENE/Uaithne
O'More	CANOC/Conmhac
	FESTUS/Fachtna
	KEDAGH/Ceadach
	ROGER/Ruaidri
O'Moriarty	CORC
	JONATHAN/Seanchen
O'Morgan	MALACHY
O'Mullin	EVENY/Aibhne
O'Mulloy	ART
O'Neill	CONN
	CULLO/Cu Ula
	ENRI/Anraoi
O'Nolan	UGHAIRE (pronounced *Uri*)
O'Quinn	NEILL/Niall
O'Reilly	FAILGHE
	GLAISNE
	MYLES
O'Rourke	ART
	CONN
	FARRELL/Fearghal
	TIARNAN
O'Shaughnessy	ROGER/Rauidri
O'Sullivan	BOETHIUS/Buadach
	FININ
O'Toole	BARNABY
	DONNCUAN
	GILKEVIN
	LORCAN
Parsons	SAVAGE
Reynolds	IOR
Trant	ION
Tyrrell	PHILPOG
Wall	ELIAS/Uilleag
Ward	MANUS

BEYOND RYAN AND MURPHY

Irish Surname Names

Two of the most popular Irish-American names, Kelly and Ryan, got their start as surnames. Another Irish surname name, Kelsey, has been zooming up the popularity charts since Ann Kelsey of "L.A. Law" used it for her baby daughter; TV's Murphy Brown has helped popularize the whole genre. And a handful of other Irish last names—Dillon, Fallon, Lacey, Redmond—have been used, however sparingly, in the United States.

But now, perhaps spurred on by the recent craze for WASPy last-names-as-first—the trendy Morgan, Jordan, Porter, Parker et al.—the Irish surname names have really come into their own. And when you consider that most Irish surnames started out as first names, taking the prefix "Mac" ("son of") or "O" ("grandson of" or "descendant of"), then it makes perfect sense to take these names back to their original forms.

While several of these names are used in Ireland for boys, in the United States most can work as well for girls' names.

For inspiration, look to your own family tree or consult this list of ambisexual choices:

BLAINE	DONOVAN
BOWIE	DUFFY
BRADY	EGAN
BRANIGAN	FALLON
BRENNAN	FARRELL
BRESLIN	FINN
BRODERICK	FITZGERALD
BRODY	FLANAGAN
BYRNE	FLANNERY
CAGNEY	FLYNN
CALHOUN	GALLAGHER
CALLAHAN	GARRITY
CASSIDY	GILLIGAN
CLANCY	GORMLEY
CONNELL	GRADY
CONNOLLY	GRIFFIN
CONNOR	HANLON
CONROY	HARRINGTON
CORCORAN	HAYES
COSTELLO	HENNESSY
CULLEN	HOGAN
CURRAN	HUGHES
DELANEY	KANE
DEMPSEY	KEARNEY
DEVLIN	KENNEDY
DILLON	KENNELLY
DOLAN	KIERNAN
DONAHUE	KINSELLA
DONEGAN	KIRBY
DONNELLY	LACEY

LENNON
LOUGHLIN
MADDEN
MAGEE
MAHONEY
MALLOY
MALONE
MANUS
McCOY
MOORE
MORRISSEY
MURROUGH
MURTAUGH
NOLAN
PHELAN
QUINLAN
QUINN
REDMOND
REGAN

REILLY/RILEY
REYNOLDS
ROONEY
ROURKE
ROWAN
SCANLON
SHAW
SHEA/SHAY
SHEEDY
SHERIDAN
SULLIVAN
SWEENEY
TALLY
TIERNEY
TULLY
TYNAN
WARD
WHELAN

BEYOND SHANNON AND KERRY

Irish Place Names

From Tipperary to Tralee, Irish place names are melodic and evocative. Two that have captured the imagination of Irish-Americans are Shannon and Kerry, but there are other less-familiar place names you may find every bit as appealing. Some of the names on this list may strike you as thoroughly feminine, others strongly masculine, but most, we think, could work well for children of either sex.

The names of Irish towns, counties, rivers, and hills, both real and imaginary, that have been or could be used for boys' or girls' first names include:

ADARE	BRAY
ARAN	CARRA
ATHEA	CARRICK
BALLINA	CARY
BANTRY	CASHEL
BRANDON	CAVAN

CLARE	KINSALE
CLIFDEN	LEENANE
CLODAGH	LOUGHLIN
CLOONE	LYSAGH/Laoiseach
CORBALLY	MAYO
CULLEN	MEADE
DERRY	MONAGHAN
DESMOND	NAVAN
DONEGAL	OOLA
DOON	PALLAS
DURROW	QUIN
EALGA	ROSS
ENNIS	SAMHAOIR
GALWAY	SCOTA
GLIN	SLANE
IERNE	SUTTON
JUVERNA	TARA
KAVANAGH	TORY
KERRY	TULLA
KILDARE	TYRONE
KILLIAN	VALENTIA

FROM KING KENNEDY OF MUNSTER TO KING KENNEDY OF MASSACHUSETTS
Names of Irish Royalty

Royalty is the last thing Irish-Americans associate with the staunch republic of Ireland, yet through the Middle Ages Ireland was teeming with rogue princes and beautiful princesses, high kings and powerful queens. This section includes the names of Irish royalty, from the infamous to the obscure, plus the names of post-royal heroes and heroines and those of that Irish-American royal family, the Kennedys.

IRISH KINGS AND QUEENS, HEROES AND HEROINES

Until the twelfth century, when the Norman invaders finally got a stronghold in Ireland and the English king Henry II declared himself the country's overlord, Ireland was ruled by high kings as well as by a number of provincial kings and queens. While many of these petty royals continued to rule for a few more centuries, the glory days of Irish kings and queens, princes and princesses were clearly on the wane.

Irish royalty was grand in its prime, however, and many of the names of the most notable kings and queens—Brian Boru, Rory O'Connor, and Grania O'Malley, to name just a few—remain well used to this day. Also, heroes of the post-royal period—Daniel O'Connell, for instance—popularized other names.

Anti-Hero Name

Oliver Cromwell's slaughter of one-quarter of the Irish-Catholic population in the 1650s, and his subsequent sale of many Irish into West Indian slavery, might have permanently turned the Irish (who despise Cromwell to this day) against the name Oliver if not for the saving grace of St. Oliver Plunkett, an Irish archbishop who was executed by the British in 1681. Had it not been for the saintly Oliver, naming a little McKenna or Connelly Oliver would have been as unthinkable as calling baby Greenberg Adolf.

If raising a little Irish prince or princess is what you have in mind, look to this list for naming inspiration:

F E M A L E

ABHLACH: An Ulster princess and mother of a king.

AFRICA: Daughter of Fergus of Galway who married Olaus the Swarthy, king of the Isle of Man.

AILBHE/Elva: Daughter of a high king and mother of a warrior-king.

AILIONORA/Eleanora: Popularized by two queen-consorts of England and introduced to Ireland by the Normans, the name was borne by several noblewomen.

AILLEANN: Two kings' mothers bore this name, which is pronounced *Alan*.

ALMATH: An early Ulster princess, whose name could be anglicized, and is pronounced *Alva*.

AOIFE: Daughter of King Dermot of Leinster who married Strongbow, leader of the Norman invasion; also the name of many other princesses.

AURNIA: Wife of Turlogh More O'Brien, thirteenth-century king.

BAILLGHEAL: A pious queen of Connacht.

BAIRRIONN: Wife of a twelfth-century Ulster king.

BEBHAILL: Queen of the high king Donnchad mac Aeda.

BEIBHINN/Bevin: Wife of Tadgh, tenth-century king of Connacht.

CAINNECH: Tenth-century princess.

CAOINTIARN: Two wives of high kings.

CEALLACH: Eighth-century princess. More common as a male name; gave rise to the surname O'Kelly.

CLODAGH: The name of a river popularized as a first name when the marquis of Waterford gave it to his daughter.

CORCAIR: A popular aristocratic name in the early Middle Ages.

COWLEY/Cobhlaith: A daughter of the powerful king Cano; also an eighth-century Leinster princess.

CRED: The name of several Irish queens and princesses, as well as of the mistress of Cano.

CRINOC: An eleventh-century Munster princess.

DAVNIT/Damhnait: Wife of a king of Munster and ancestress of the O'Moriartys, O'Cahills, O'Flynns, and O'Carrolls.

DERVAL/Dearbhail: The name of several medieval queens and princesses.

DERVOGILLA: The wife of Tiernan O'Rourke, king of Breifne; she eloped with Dermot McMurrough, king of Leinster, but later repented and became a nun.

DEVASSE: A daughter of Amlaib O'Donoghue, who founded the fortunes of the O'Donoghue family.

DOIREANN/Dorren: The mother of Gilla Patraic, an eleventh-century king.

DUIBHLEAMHNA: Daughter of a king and wife of a high king.

DUNLA/Dunlaith: Wife of the high king Niall Frassach as well as the name of daughters of two high kings.

EACHRA: A tenth-century princess noted for her beautiful complexion.

EAVAN/Aoibhinn: The name of several princesses, including a daughter of the royal prince of Tara who died in the tenth century.

EIBHLIN: A popular aristocratic name in Northern Ireland. It was brought to Ireland by the Normans in the forms Avelina and Emeline; is identical with the English Evelina and Evelyn; and—while it achieved popularity as Eibhlin—has been retranslated as Eileen, Aileen, and other variations.

EITHNE: The name of several early queens and princesses.

FAILENN: An early Cashel princess.

FARVILA/Forlaith: A princess who became an abbess.

FINNEACHT: A princess of Meath and the mother of a saint.

FLANN: The name of two famous early queens.

GORMLAITH/Gormley: The name of several early and well-known queens, including the wife of high king Brian Boru who was also a daughter of the king of Leinster and the mother of Sitric, king of Dublin.

GRANIA/Grainne: Grania Mhaoel Ni Mhaolmhaigh, or Grace O'Malley, was the sixteenth-century queen of the Western Isles of Ireland.

LASSAR: An early princess.

LIOCH: The daughter of one high king and wife of an-other.

MAOL MHUADH: The name of several wives and daughters of kings and high kings; it is pronounced *Melvira*.

MOR: The name of several queens of Ireland.

MUIRGEL: The name of several queens of Ireland.

NARVLA/Narbhla: The daughter of a prince and the wife of an abbot.

PATRICIA: Princess of Connaught.

RANALT: Daughter of Awley O'Farrell, king of Conmacne, and wife of Hugh O'Connor, twelfth-century king of Connaught.

RONAIT: The daughter of a high king.

SEADACH: An eleventh-century princess.

SIVE/Sadb: Daughter of Brian Boru.

TAILLTE: Daughter of the king of Meath and wife of high king Turlough O'Connor.

TARA/Temair: The wife of a seventh-century high king.

TUATHLA: An early queen of Leinster.

UALLACH: Chief poetess of Ireland in the tenth century. Pronounced *Wallach*.

M A L E

AILILL: Ailill Molt, an early king.

AINMIRE: Sixth-century king of Tara.

AODH/Hugh: The name of many kings and nobles, including three high kings. Also the name of two famous Irish rebels who lived in Elizabethan times: Aodh (or Hugh) O'Neill and Aodh Rua (Red Hugh) O'Donnell.

ART: Art McMurrough, medieval king of Leinster.

AWLEY: Awley O'Farrell, king of Conmacne.

BAODAN: The name of two powerful sixth-century kings.

BLATHMAC: A seventh-century king of Tara.

BRANDUFF/Brandubh: A medieval king of Leinster.

BREASAL: An early Leinster king.

BRIAN: Name of the most famous high king of Ireland, Brian Boru, who defeated the Norse.

CAILLIN: An early prince who was ancestor to a dynasty of Cork kings.

CALLAGHAN: A tenth-century king of Munster.

CANO: A seventh-century king of Scotland and Ireland.

CATHAL: The name of a thirteenth-century king of Connacht, Cathal Crobhlhearg, as well as the Irish Civil War patriot Cathal Brugha.

CEARUL: The name of a great warrior-king and of many noblemen of Leinster.

CEAT: King of Corcumroe; pronounced *Cat.*

CONALL: Conall Cernach was a great Ulster hero.

CONCHOBAR: Conchobar mac Nessa was king of Ulster.

CONNELL/Congal: A seventh-century Ulster king and an eighth-century high king.

CORMAC: Cormac MacCuilleanan, bishop and king of Munster. Also the name of several other kings as well as the legendary ancestors of the O'Neills, O'Briens, and MacNamaras.

CORMACAN: One of the chief poets of medieval Ireland.

CRIONAN: An eleventh-century king and an ancestor of the O'Falveys.

CRUINN: An early king of Ulaid and the founder of a dynasty.

CUAN: An early king; also an eleventh-century poet.

CUANA: An early warrior and the king of Fermoy.

DAHY (Daithi): A king of Tara.

DALLAN: Two famous early poets.

DANIEL: Daniel O'Connell, early nineteenth-century lawyer who campaigned for Catholic emancipation and was known as The Liberator.

DEAMAN: An early Ulster king.

DERMOT: Dermot MacMurrough, the twelfth-century Leinster king, who invited the Normans into Ireland.

DONAGH/Donnchadh: High King Donagh, son of Brian Boru.

DONAL: The name of five high kings.

DUNLANG: The name of two early kings, one who was an ancestor of the O'Donoghues and another who was an ancestor of the O'Tooles and O'Byrnes.

EMMET: Robert Emmet was an eighteenth-century rebel.

EOCHAID: An early Irish king, Eochaid Mugmedon, whose name means "Lord of the Slaves."

FAELAN: The name of three kings of Leinster between the seventh and ninth centuries.

FELIM: A medieval king of Connacht.

FERGUS: The name of several early kings.

FIACH: Fiach MacHugh O"Beirne was a sixteenth-century Irish rebel who fought the English.

FINGUINE: The name of two early Munster kings.

FLAITHRI: An early king; also an archbishop of Tuam and a distinguished ecclesiastic and writer.

FLANN: A distinguished name borne by a king; a high king, who was an ancestor of the O'Connors; and several famous early poets.

GLASSAN: An early Ulster prince.

GORMAN: A king of Munster and an ancestor of the O'Keefes.

GUAIRE: A king of Connacht famed for his generosity.

JACK: Jack Cade, an Irishman who in the fifteenth century led an uprising in England.

KENNEDY: King Kennedy of Munster, father of Brian Boru.

KENNELLY: The principal poet of Munster.

KENNETH/Cinaed: An eighth-century high king.

LACHTNA/Lucius: The name of several early kings and nobles, including the brother and the great-grandfather of Brian Boru.

LAOGHAIRE: A king of Tara.

LENNAN: An early king.

LORCAN: The name of several kings, including the grandfather of Brian Boru.

MAHON: Brian Boru's brother and a tenth-century king of Cashel.

MALACHY: The name of two famous high kings of Ireland.

MUIRIOS: A favorite name among noble Connacht families.

MURTAGH: The name of three kings of Tara, as well as of the prince called Muircheartach of the Leather Cloak.

NIALL: King of Tara, Niall of the Nine Hostages, who founded the Ui Neill dynasty of Irish kings; also Niall Black-Knee, founder of the O'Neill family, who died fighting the Norse in the tenth century.

PATRICK: Patrick Pearse, the rebel leader of 1916, who reinforced the popularity of the name introduced by St. Patrick.

RORY: Rory O'Conor, who ruled 1166–1170, was the last high king of Ireland. Rory O'More was a seventeenth-century Irish patriot.

RUMANN: A great early poet.

SCANNLAN: An early king.

SHANE: An Elizabethan-era Irish prince, Shane the Proud, who was chief of the O'Neill family.

SITRIC: The name of several kings of Dublin in the Middle Ages, most notably Sitric Silkenbeard.

SUIBNE: An early high king. Pronounced *Sweeney*.

TADHG: The name of several kings.

TIBBOT: The son of Grania or Grace O'Malley, Tibbot of the Ship was so called because he was born at sea.

TURLOUGH: The name of two kings, Turlough I O'Brien and Turlough II O'Conor, who ruled in the tenth and eleventh centuries.

IRISH-AMERICAN ROYALTY

Kennedy Names

Ireland had King Kennedy of Munster, father of Brian Boru. And America had King Kennedy of Massachusetts, father of the princely John-John. The Kennedys are the closest thing to an Irish-American royal family, and their story, like those of the Irish kings and queens, is rife with drama and tragedy, fairy-tale heroes and falls from grace.

While the Kennedys' names may not be as interesting as their exploits, they nonetheless hold a certain fascination for expectant parents who grew up comparing themselves to Caroline and John-John. The Kennedy names are also interesting in terms of Irish-American naming trends: Among the youngest generation of Kennedys, for instance, there's one granddaughter with the very Irish name Maeve—a legendary queen's name at that; another grandchild, Caroline's first child, who's named after great-grandma Rose; and several who have Irish surname names as middle names. What we're waiting for is a Kennedy grandchild with the first name Kennedy: Kennedy Shlossberg? Kennedy Schwarzenegger? King Kennedy the II, or, if you count the Irish one, the III?

Here are the names of former president John F. Kennedy's family: his name as well as those of his siblings, their children, and their grandchildren. First and middle names only are included; the family names (like Kennedy and Hartington and Taylor) noted here are middle names, not surnames.

K E N N E D Y   S I B L I N G S

F E M A L E

EUNICE MARY   PATRICIA
JEAN ANN   ROSEMARY
KATHLEEN

M A L E

EDWARD MOORE   JOSEPH PATRICK, JR.
JOHN FITZGERALD   ROBERT FRANCIS

K E N N E D Y   K I D S

F E M A L E

AMANDA MARY   KATHLEEN HART-
CAROLINE BOUVIER   INGTON
KARA ANNE   KYM MARIA

MARIA OWINGS
MARY COURTNEY
MARY KERRY
ROBIN ELIZABETH

RORY ELIZABETH
  KATHERINE
SYDNEY MALEIA
VICTORIA FRANCES

M A L E

ANTHONY PAUL
CHRISTOPHER
CHRISTOPHER
  GEORGE
DAVID ANTHONY
DOUGLAS HARRI-
  MAN
EDWARD MOORE,
  JR.
JOHN FITZGERALD,
  JR.
JOSEPH PATRICK II
MARK KENNEDY

MATTHEW MAX-
  WELL TAYLOR
MICHAEL LeMOYNE
PATRICK JOSEPH
ROBERT FRANCIS,
  JR.
ROBERT SARGENT
  III
STEPHEN EDWARD,
  JR.
TIMOTHY PERRY
WILLIAM KENNEDY

K E N N E D Y   K I D S '   K I D S

G I R L S

ALEXANDRA
CAROLINE
KATHERINE EUNICE
KYLE FRANCES

MAEVE FAHEY
MEAGHAN ANN
RORY
ROSE KENNEDY

ROSE POTTER   TATIANA CELIA
SAVANNAH ROSE

B O Y S

CHRISTOPHER   PATRICK
DAVID CHRISTO-   PETER
  PHER   ROBERT FRANCIS III
JOSEPH PATRICK III   TIMOTHY POTTER
MATTHEW RAUCH
MICHAEL LeMOYNE,
  JR.

FROM ST. PATRICK TO ST. ATTRACTA

Irish Saints' Names

IRISH SAINTS' NAMES

Judging from the length of this list of names, it seems as if every second person walking around Ireland in the fifth, sixth, and seventh centuries must have been a saint. In fact, Ireland was a center of religious learning and fervor in those long-ago days, and sainthoods were also more generously conferred.

Many of the names on this list do not appear anywhere else in the book; they live on only through the religious notoriety of their most famous bearers and are otherwise obsolete. And honestly, what's a modern parent supposed to do with a name like Bigseach, or Mo Bi, other than use it to torture his or her spouse?

There are several saints' names, however, that are lovely and still used widely for twentieth-century children. There are others that have fallen out of use but may still strike a euphonic chord in some modern parents' ears. The trick is to find them: Hunting for a good name for your child on this list can be like searching for a Chanel suit in a giant thrift store. You may find one, but you'll have to sift through an awful lot of stained polyester blouses first.

Of course, this list can be useful for any parents whose religious beliefs dictate choosing a saint's name for their child. But bear in mind that many widely used Irish names—Aisling, Deirdre, Finola, Maeve, Brian, Connor, and Rory, to name just a few—are not saints' names but were popularized by ancient kings, queens, and mythological figures. Just because a name is Irish, in other words, doesn't make it Catholic.

With that in mind, here is a list of the names of Irish saints:

F E M A L E

AIDEEN/Etaoin	CAOMHOG
AINE	CEARA
AINFEAN	CEALLSACH
AITHCHE	CIANNAIT
ALMA	CIAR
ATTRACTA	CLORA/Clothra
BANBHNAIT	COLUMBA
BARRAN	COMNAIT
BIGSEACH	CONNA
BLATH	CORBACH
BLINNE	CORBNAIT
BRECCNAT	CRANAIT
BRIGH	CRAOBHNAIT
BRIGIT	CRON
BRIUINSEACH	CRONSECH
CAINNEAR	CRUIMSEACH
CAIREACH	CUACH
CAOIMSEACH	CUACHNAIT
CAOMHNAIT	CUMMAN

CURCHACH
DAGHAIN
DAIRE
DAIRILE
DAREARCA
DEARLU
DERVILA/Deirbhile
DOMINICA
DUINSEACH
DYMPHNA/Damhnait
EARCNAIT
EAVNAT/Aobhnait
EIRNIN
EITHNE
ENAT/Aodhnait
ESCRACH
ETAIN
FAINCHE
FAINNEAR
FAOILEANN
FEAMAIR
FEENAT/Fianait
FEME
FIDELMA/Fedelm
FINNAT
FINNEACHT
FINNECH
FINNSEACH
FLANNAIT
GOBNAIT
GORMLAITH
INA/Aghna
ITA

KEAVY/Caoimhe
KEELIN/Caolinn
LAIMHSEACH
LAITHCHE
LALLOC
LASAIR
LIADAN
LOIMSEACH
LUCY/Luiseach
MIONAIT
MONA(T)/Muadhnait
MUGHAIN
NEACHT
ORNA(T)
OSNAIT
PHIALA
RATHNAIT
RIOFACH
RIONA/Rionach
ROINSEACH
RONAIT
RUADHNAIT
SAMTHANN
SARNAIT
SCIATH
SCOTH
SEANAIT
SEARC
SUAIBHSEACH
TALULLA/Tuilelaith
TARA/Teamhair
TUILEACH
UASAL

M A L E

ABAN	BRENDAN/Breanainn
ACOBHRAN	BRICIN
ADOMNAN	BROGAN
AENGUS	BRONE
AIDAN/Aodhan	CAILLIN
AILBHE	CAIMIN
AILILL	CAIRBRE
AILITHIR	CAIREALL
AINMIRE	CAIRNEACH
AMHALGAIDH	CALLAGHAN
ANFUDAN	CANICE/Cainneach
AOIDHGHEAN	CAOLAN
AOLU	CAOLBHADH
AONA	CAOMHAN
BAIRRIONN	CARTHAGE/Carthach
BANBHAN	CASS
BAODAN	CASSAIR
BAOITHIN	CASSAN
BEANON	CATHAN
BEARACH	CIANAN
BEARCHAN	COLE
BEC	COLGA
BECCAN	COLMAN
BLAMHAC	COLUMBA
BRAN	COLUMBCILLE
BRANDUFF/Brandubh	COMAN
BRAON	CONALL
BRAZIL	CONAN
BRECC	CONLEY/Conlao
BRECCAN	CONNLA

CONUIL
CORC
CORCAN
CORCORAN
CORMAC
COWAL/Comhghall
COWAN/Comhghan
CREEDON/Criodan
CREMIN/Cruimin
CRONAN
CUAN
CUMMIAN/Cuimin
CURNAN
DAGHAN
DAIGH
DAIGHRE
DAIRE
DALBHACH
DALLAN
DAVIN/Damhan
DECLAN
DERMOT/Diarmaid
DIANACH
DICUILL
DIMMA
DINEARTACH
DIOCHU
DIOMAN
DONAL/Domnall
DONNAN
DOWD/Dubhda
DUBHAN
DUFFY/Dufach

DUNCHADH
EARC
EILTIN
EIRNIN
ELAIR
ENAN
ENDA/EANNA
EOCHAID
EOGHANAN
EVAN/Eimhin
FACHTNA
FAILBHE
FAIRCHEALLACH
FALLON/Faithleann
FANAHAN/Finnchu
FAOILTIARN
FAOLAN
FAOLCHU
FEARDOMHNACH
FEICHIN
FELIM(ID)
FERGAL
FERGUS
FETHCHU
FETHMAC
FIACC
FIACHNA
FIACHRA
FINAN
FININ
FINNAN
FIN(N)BAR
FINNCHAD

FINNCHAN
FINNEACHTA
FINNIAN
FINNLUG
FINTAN
FLANN
FLANNAN
FORANNAN
FORTCHERN
FRAOCHAN
FRASSACH
FURSEY/Fursa
GALL
GARVIN
GILLESPIE/Giolla
   Easpaig
GLASAN
GOBAN
GREALLAN
GRIFFIN/Criofan
GUAIRE
GUASACHT
HIERO
HUGH/Aodh
IARLUGH
IMCHAD
IOMHAR
IVAR/Iobhar
JARLATH/Iarlaith
KELLY/Cellach
KENNELLY/Cionnaola
KEVIN/Caoimhin
KIERAN/Ciaran

KILIAN/Cillin
LACHTIN
LAIDHGEANN
LAOBHAN
LASERIAN/Laisren
LEANAN/Liadhnan
LEARY/Laoghaire
LIBER
LITHGEN
LOCHAN
LOMAN
LONAN
LORAN/Luaran
LORCAN
LUGHAN
LUGHNA
LUI
LUITHIARN
MACARTAN
MacCOILLE
MacCUILIND
MacDARA
MacLAISRE
MacNISSE
MacTAIL
MAEDOC
MALACHY/
   Maolmhaodhog
MALCOLM
MALONE/Maol Eoin
MANCHAN
MANNIX/Mainchin
MANY/Maine

MAOLANAITHE
MAOLORAIN
MAONACH
MARCAN
MARIANUS/Maol
  Mhuire
MEALLAN
MEL
MICHAN
MO BI
MOCHAOMHOG
MOCHOLLA
MOCHONNA
MOCHTA
MOCHUA
MOCHUDA
MOCHUMA
MOLAISSE
MOLUA
MUADHAN
MUIRIN
MUNA
MURA
MURCHU
MURRAY/Muirioch
NANNID
NATHY/Naithi
NEACHTAN
NEAMH
NESSAN
NUADHA
OILLEOG

OLAN/Eolann
ONCHU
ORAN
OSAN
OSSIAN/Oisin
OWEN/Eoan
PATRICK/Padraig
RIAGHAIL
RODAN
RONAN
ROSS
ROWAN/Ruadhan
RUISIN
RYAN/Rian
SANCTAN
SARAN
SCOITHIN
SEADNA
SEANAN
SEIGHIN
SIOLLAN
SLEIBHIN
SUIBHNE
TASSACH
TEIMHNIN
TIARNACH
TIARNAN
TOLA
TOMMAN
TUAMA
ULTAN
ZEPHAN

HOLIER BY THE DOZEN

To multiply further the number of Irish saints, there are several saint names that count more than one saint to their credit. A lot more than one if ancient Irish records can be believed, for there are the following number of saints with these names:

COLMAN 234
FINTAN 74
MOCHUA 59
MOLAISSE 46
MOLUA 38
MOCHUMA 33
COLUMBA 32
MOCHONNA 29
KIERAN/Ciaran 26
AIDAN/Aodhan 21
MOCHAOMHOG 21

HUGH/Aodh 20
LIBER 18
BRENDAN/Breanainn 17
BRIGIT 15
FAOLAN 14
BRECCAN 13
BRIGH 13
MOCHOLLA 13

CONAN, PATRON SAINT OF BARBARIANS

—And Other Patron Saints You May Not Have Heard Of

The Irish Saint MacDara is the patron saint of fishermen. Fiachra is the patron saint of cabdrivers. St. Aodh (Hugh) Mac Bricc is the patron saint of headache sufferers. This much we're not making up. St. Conan's patronage of barbarians, however, is purely our flight of fancy, as are the following, inspired by the names:

ATTRACTA, patron saint of beauty products

BRAZIL, patron saint of samba dancers

FLANN, patron saint of crème caramel

LOMAN, patron saint of traveling salesmen

MANNIX, patron saint of TV detectives

MO BI, patron saint of whales

MURRAY and MEL, patron saints of deli owners

RYAN, patron saint of men with girlfriends named Farrah

TARA, patron saint of plantations

LIVING SAINTS

To simplify the task of the parent who's looking for an Irish name that's used in modern times and is also a saint's name, we've compiled the following list. One caveat: these are by no means all the interesting and usable names on the overall list of saints, just the ones that are still in general circulation. These names include:

FEMALE

AIDEEN	EAVNAT
AINE	EITHNE
ALMA	ETAIN
BLINNE	FAINCHE
BRIGIT	FIDELMA
CEARA	GOBNAIT
DERVILA	GORMLAITH
DOMINICA	INA
DYMPHNA	ITA

KEAVY
KEELIN
LUCY
MONA(T)

ORNA(T)
RIONA
TALULLA
TARA

M A L E

AENGUS
AIDAN
BRENDAN
BROGAN
CALLAGHAN
CANICE
COLE
COLMAN
CONALL
CONLEY
CORCORAN
DECLAN
DERMOT/Diarmaid
DONAL
DUFFY
EVAN
FALLON
FELIM(ID)
FERGUS
FIN(N)BAR
FINNIAN
FINTAN
FLANN
GARVIN

GRIFFIN
HUGH
KELLY (usually for
  girls)
KENNELLY
KEVIN
KIERAN
KILIAN
LORAN
LORCAN
MACARTAN
MALACHY
MALCOLM
MALONE
MEL
MURRAY
OWEN
PATRICK
RONAN
ROSS
ROWAN
RYAN
TIARNAN

Non-Irish Saints

There are some saints who, while not actually Irish, may as well be, considering the great influence they've had on the names of Irish-Catholic children. Irish holy men and women who traveled abroad and foreign missionaries who visited Ireland imported these names and popularized them from the early Middle Ages on. The most notable of these non-Irish saints' names is, of course, Patrick, Ireland's patron saint and its "national name" (see page 34). But other biblical and ecclesiastical luminaries have provided much naming inspiration as well. These saints' names include:

G I R L S

ABIGAIL
AGNES
ANNE

BERNADETTE
CATHERINE/
    KATHERINE

CECILIA
CLARE
JOAN
MARGARET
MARTHA

PATRICIA
PHILOMENA
T(H)ERESA
VERONICA

B O Y S

ADAM
BERNARD
DANIEL
DOMINIC
FRANCIS
IGNATIUS
JAMES
JOHN
JOSEPH

MARTIN (of Tours)
MICHAEL
NICHOLAS
STEPHEN
THOMAS (apostle and
à Becket)
TIMOTHY
VINCENT

FROM FINN
MacCOOL TO
SINEAD
O'CONNOR
Famous Irish Names

The Irish are world famous for their stories and their music, and many of the Irish names that live on in America as well as Ireland were popularized by mythical and literary characters, by both the singers and their songs. In this section, the famous names of Irish myth, legend, literature, song, and stardom: from the great hero Finn MacCool to the characters in *Finnegan's Wake*; from Sweet Molly Malone to bald Sinead O'Connor.

Names from Irish Myth and Legend

Ireland is rich in folk tales and legends starring characters that range from pagan gods and goddesses to ancient kings and queens to the fairies who live in the roots of old trees. But perhaps the greatest Irish legends of them all center on the mythical hero Finn MacCool, son of a slain warrior and a king's daughter, whose maternal grandfather tries to drown him the day he's born. The infant Finn MacCool surfaces from his watery fate holding a salmon in his hand and is raised by his paternal grandmother in a cave with the dog Bran. He grows up to become a great warrior with mystical powers, derived from chewing his fingers, literally, to the bone. After using his magic to save the king's horse, he rejects the reward of the princess' hand in marriage and asks instead for the lives of the condemned champions of Erin. These champions become the followers of Finn, the first Fenians, or Fianna, of Ireland.

Many of the Irish names of myth that remain the most popular and appealing come from the Fenian legends. There's the princess Niamh, who ran away with Finn Mac-

Cool's son, Ossian; Grania, Finn's sweetheart, who eloped with Dermot; and Aine, who refused to sleep with any man but Finn. And on the male side, there's Dermot, Conan, Ossian, and of course Finn MacCool himself, who, besides being the quintessential hero, has what must be the ultimate hero name.

Some other names of Irish legend survive as well: Deirdre, for instance, Eithne, Maeve, and Una for girls; Conor, Cormac, and Ronan for boys. And there are names that survive only in legend that deserve to be revived: Caireann, Ceara, Daire, and Glas are notable for their melodic qualities; and other names may inspire you because of their associations with mythical characters or events.

Still, many of the names that follow should perhaps stay confined to legend. It's difficult to imagine a modern child going through life with the name Blathnat, for example, or Abhartach or Cuchulainn.

Here, for inspiration or maybe just for edification, is a who's who of Irish myth and legend:

F E M A L E

ACHALL: Daughter of the legendary warrior Cairbre Nia Fer; she died of sorrow when her brother was killed.

AI: Ai the Arrogant, daughter of Finn, who refused to marry any man who wasn't Irish. In keeping with her egotistical identity, her name is pronounced *I*.

AIBELL: A pagan name of one of the ancient Irish goddesses. In various stories, she is the fairy who appears to Brian Boru on the eve of battle, the daughter of a warrior, and the daughter of a king of Munster.

AILBHE: One legendary Ailbhe was a daughter of the fairy

king Midir; another was a daughter of Cormac mac Art and one of the four best lovers in Ireland. Ailbhe is pronounced, and anglicized, *Elva*.

AINE: The name of many legendary heroines: a fairy-queen; lover of the sea god who took her to the Land of Promise; daughter of the king of Scotland who would sleep with no man but Finn, whom she married and with whom she bore two sons. The name, which remains popular in Ireland, is pronounced *Anya*.

AINNIR: A character in the Finn tales.

BAINE: Daughter of the legendary ancestor of Ireland's kings.

BANBHA: The name of an early Irish goddess.

BEARRACH: A character of legendary generosity, and the third wife of Finn.

BEIBHINN: One legendary Beibhinn was daughter of the king of the Otherworld; another Beibhinn was the mother of the hero slain by Cuchulainn. It is pronounced, and anglicized, *Bevin*.

BINN: A fairy-woman.

BLATHNAT: Wife of a West Munster hero, she betrayed her husband and was killed by his poet.

BOINN: Wife and mother of gods; goddess of the Boyne.

BUANANN: A goddess; also a mother who tutored warriors in arms.

CAINNLEACH: Foster mother of an Ulster hero, she died of sorrow when her son was slain.

CAIRREAN: Daughter of the king of the Britons, mother of Niall of the Nine Hostages, and legendary ancestress of the high kings of Ireland. Pronounced *Karen*.

CATHACH: A legendary female warrior.

CEIBHIONN: Daughter of a fairy. Pronounced *Kevin*.

CEARA: Wife of a legendary invader of Ireland; pronounced *Cara*.

CIARNAIT: Mistress of the legendary king Cormac mac Art.

CLIDNA: The name of three mythical heroines: a Tuatha de Danann, who gave her name to one of the three great waves of Ireland; one of the three beautiful daughters of Libra, poet to the sea god; and a fairy-woman to the MacCarthy clan.

CLOTHRA: Sister of legendary queen Maeve, whose name is pronounced and can be anglicized as *Clora*.

COCHRANN: Mother of Dermot, the greatest lover in Irish legend, who eloped with Grania, Finn MacCool's beloved.

CRED: The name of several legendary queens and princesses, most notably the daughter of Cairbre, king of Ciarraige, who fell in love with the warrior Cael and died of sorrow when he was slain in battle. The name is pronounced *Cree*.

CROCHNAIT: Mother of the Fenians Dermot and Oscar.

DAIRINE:The daughter of a legendary king.

DANA: Pagan goddess who bestowed her name on the Tuatha De Danaan, the legendary early inhabitants of Ireland.

DAROVA: A legendary princess.

DEIRDRE: Heroine of the tragic legend, she was betrothed to the king of Ulster but eloped with one of the three sons of Uisneach, all of whom were then killed by the king.

DELLA: Came to Ireland in a legendary invasion.

DOIREANN: Daughter of the fairy king Midir. An English form is Dorren.

DRAIGEN: Wife of the legendary ancestor of the kings of Munster.

DUNLA: Daughter of the warrior Regamon.

EACHNA: Daughter of a king, she was reputed to be one of most beautiful and intelligent women in the world. Pronounced *Ahkna.*

EACHTACH: A daughter of the great lovers Grania and Dermot.

EILE: Sister of Queen Maeve.

EITHNE: One of the most popular names of legend. Eithne was, variously, mother of the god Lug, wife of Conn of the Hundred Battles, and wife of Cormac mac Art. The name is pronounced *Enna,* and has been anglicized as Anne, Annie, and Ena.

EMER: Wife of the hero Cuchulainn. Pronounced *Ever.*

EORANN: A legendary queen. Pronounced *Oran.*

ERNE: A princess after whom Lough Erne is named.

ETAIN: A lover of Midir, a male fairy.

ETAN: The name of Cuchulainn's mistress as well as of the daughter of the mythical god of healing. The modern Irish spelling is Eadan.

EVA: A wife of Nemed, legendary invader of Ireland; also, a Fenian heroine who was drowned at sea. The modern Irish spelling, Eabha, only confuses the pronunciation.

EVEGREN: Daughter of the tragic Deirdre and Noise.

EVLIN/Eibhleann: A mythical spirit who gave her name to a mountain range.

FAIFE: Daughter of Ailill and Queen Maeve.

FAILENN: A princess and the mother of Eithne, wife of the king of Cashel.

FAINCHE: One name of the Irish goddess of war; also a mythical saint who, when threatened with marriage, jumped into Lough Erne and swam underwater to the sea. The name is anglicized as, and sounds similar to, *Fanny.*

FANN: Wife of the sea god.

FETHNAT: Musician to the Tuatha de Danann.

FIAL: Wife of the founder of the O'Driscoll and O'Coffey families; also the name of Emer's sister and of a goddess.

FIDELMA/Fedelm: The name of several legendary queens, princesses, and great beauties.

FINNABAIR: A daughter of Queen Maeve and Ailill. This name is related to the Welsh Guinevere and therefore Jennifer. An English equivalent is Fennore.

FINNCHAEM: Alternately, the wife of Cian; the mother of the hero Conall Cearnach; and the daughter of one fairy king and the wife of another.

FINNCHNES: In the Finn stories, the daughter of a king and also a robe-maker for the Fianna.

FINSCOTH: Cuchulainn's daughter.

FITHIR: The daughter of a legendary king.

FLIDAIS: Daughter of Ailill Finn, the legendary Connacht king, she fell in love with an exiled warrior.

FODLA: Wife of the god Mac Cecht whose name is another name for Ireland. The "d" is silent.

GELACE/Geileis: The daughter of a legendary king of Connacht.

GRANIA: Finn MacCool's betrothed, who eloped with Dermot.

GRIAN: A daughter of Finn MacCool.

ISEULT: Irish princess who was the lover of Tristan in the Arthurian legend.

IUCHRA: She turned Aoife, her rival, into a heron.

LIADAN: Mother of St. Ciaran who, according to legend, conceived him when a star fell in her mouth.

LOCH: Daughter of a legendary warrior and mother of a legendary poet.

LONNOG: She was kind to Mad Sweeney, the mythical wild bird-man.

LUGACH: A daughter of Finn MacCool.

MACHA: A war goddess of the Tuatha de Danann; another legendary Macha is called "Macha of the red hair."

MAEN: Daughter of Conn of the Hundred Battles; another Maen was a king's daughter and mother of a legendary judge. Pronounced *men*.

MAEVE: The legendary queen of Connacht who led an invasion of Ulster.

MARGO: The mother of the beautiful Etain.

MELL: The legendary mother of seven saints.

MONCHA: A pagan goddess.

MONGFIND: One Mongfind was daughter of king of the Picts; another Mongfind was a daughter of the king of Scotland and Ireland.

MUGAIN: The name of a queen or goddess.

MUIREACHT: The wife of the king of Tara.

MUIREANN: Name of the foster mother of Cael and also of the wife of Ossian. Pronounced *Mearan*.

MUIRIN: Lived for three hundred years in Lough Neagh.

MUIRNE: The mother of Finn MacCool.

NEAMHAIN: An ancient war goddess. Pronounced *Navin*.

NESS: Mother of Conchobar.

NIAMH: Princess of the Land of Promise who left with Finn MacCool's son Ossian for the Otherworld.

SAMHAOIR: A daughter of Finn MacCool.

SARAID: A legendary ancestress of the people of Muskerry and of the kings of Scotland.

SCATHACH: A female warrior and the teacher of Cuchulainn; another Scathach lulls Finn to sleep with magic music.

SCOTA: The name of two progenitors of the Irish race, the wife of Niul and the wife of Milesius.

SIVE/Sadb: Daughter of Conn of the Hundred Battles and wife of the legendary Munster king Ailill. Another Sive was a daughter of Queen Maeve.

SUANACH: Sister of Finn MacCool and mother of the warrior Fiachra.

TAILLTE: A mythical nurse; also the daughter of a legendary king of Spain. The Latinized version of the name is Taltena.

TARA/Temhair: A mythical character after whom the Hill of Tara is named.

TEFFIA/Teafa: A mythical princess.

TEIDE: A wife of Finn MacCool.

UAINE: In the Finn tales, she makes beautiful music.

UNA: Daughter of a legendary king of Lachlainn and the mother of Conn of the Hundred Battles.

M A L E

ABHARTACH: Father of the Fenian warrior Cael's beloved.

AENGUS: Aengus of the Birds was the god of love among the pagan Irish.

AILBHE: The name of twelve warriors of the Fianna. Another mythical Ailbhe went seeking the Land of Promise.

AILILL: A warrior who fought a battle with the legendary Fothad, who had stolen his wife.

AIMIRGIN: The first poet of Ireland.

AINLE: An early sun god. Also, one of the three brothers who were slain by the king of Ulster, after he eloped with Dierdre.

ALAN: Celtic god, brother of Bran.

AMALGITH: A man whose seven sons were baptized by St. Patrick.

BRAN: A Celtic god; also, the name of two Fenian warriors as well as of Finn MacCool's dog.

BREAS: A popular name in myth and legend.

BRION: A name often found in very early legends.

CADHAN: A legendary hero who, with his dog, killed a monster. The name is pronounced, and anglicized, *Kyne.*

CAEL: A fallen Fenian hero.

CAILTE: A Fenian warrior famous for being swift of foot. Pronounced *kilty.*

CAIRBRE: There are two legendary Cairbres: one was the son of Cormac mac Art; another Cairbre was the son of Niall of the Nine Hostages.

CASS: A legendary ancestor of the Dal Cais, from whom the families O'Brien, MacNamara, and O'Grady sprang.

CATHAIR: A legendary king of Leinster who had thirty-three sons.

CETHERN: A name for the god of the Otherworld; also father of a famous mythical Druid.

CIAN: The name of two legendary heroes. Cian has been anglicized as Kean (which reflects its pronounciation), King, and—inaccurately—Cain.

CIONNAOLA: In early law legends, a hero who remembered every word he learned at law school and wrote it down to form the earliest written record of Irish law. It can be anglicized, and is pronounced, *Kennelly.*

CLOTHACH: Grandson of Dagda, the imperial god.

CONAIRE: A legendary high king. This name is pronounced *Connery*.

CONALL: The name of many legendary kings and heroes, sometimes anglicized as Connell.

CONAN: Conan the Bald, one of the Fianna.

CONN: The name of a legendary king, Conn of the Hundred Battles, who is supposed to have been an ancestor of many famous families, including the O'Neills, the O'Donnells, the O'Rourkes, and the O'Connors.

CONOR: Conor mac Nessa, mythological king of Ulster.

CORMAC: Legendary king of Tara, Cormac Mac Art, who was ancestor of the O'Neills.

CRIOFAN: The name of several legendary kings and warriors, pronounced to rhyme with *Griffin*.

CUCHULAINN: The greatest of all the Irish warriors.

CUMHAL: The father of Finn MacCool or MacCumhail, Cumhal Mac Art was a king and champion of the west of Ireland, whose death in a battle the day after his marriage was foretold by a Druid.

DAGDA: An imperial pagan god and leader of the legendary early inhabitants of Ireland.

DAIRE: An early fertility god.

DERMOT: A hero of Irish legend who eloped with Grania, the betrothed of Finn MacCool.

DOCTOR: Name given to the seventh son of a seventh son, who is said to have healing powers.

DONN: The god of the dead.

EHIR/Aicher: A musician of the Fianna.

EIBHEAR: The son of Milesius.

ENNAE: A legendary king of Munster.

EOCHAID: An extremely popular name in legend. One Eochaid was a lover of the fairy Etain.

FEDELMID: The name of several legendary and mythological heroes, including the ancestor of the O'Neills.

FERADACH: The name of several kings of legend.

FERGUS: Fergus mac Erca, legendary leader of the Gaels' migration from Ireland to Scotland in the fifth century.

FIA: A son of Finn MacCool.

FIACHNA: The son of a mythical sea god.

FINN: Finn MacCool or MacCumhail, the greatest legendary hero of them all: leader of the Fianna; father of the master poet Ossian; spurned lover of Grania.

FITHEL: A legendary judge; also, a brother of Finn.

FRAECH: The son of a fairy-woman and the handsomest man in Ireland.

GAEL: Hero for whom the Irish race is named.

GLAS: Glas Mac Aonchearda, a Fenian and follower of Finn MacCool.

INSIN: The foster son of Finn MacCool, who was killed by the Greeks while defending Finn against them.

LABHRAIDH: Labhraidh (pronounced *Lowry*) of the Red Hand was a Fenian hero who traveled with Oscar.

LOCH: A mythological ancestor of Ireland's kings.

LUGH: Tuatha De Danaan hero who killed Balor of the Evil Eye.

MATHA: A Tuatha de Danann Druid.

MIACH: Son of the pagan god Diancecht.

MIDIR: Fairy son of the god Dagda and lover of Etain.

MILESIUS: A legendary leader of the Milesians or Celts into Ireland.

MORANN: A legendary judge who always judged correctly; also ten Fenian warriors.

MOROLT: Brother of Iseult, Tristan's doomed lover.

NOISE: Deirdre's tragic lover. Pronounced *nice*.

NUADU: God of the Otherworld; the fisher-god.

OSCAR: A hero; Finn MacCool's grandson.

OSSIAN: The son of Finn MacCool and a woman who sometimes transmogrified into a deer, he lived for a while in the Land of Promise.

PARTHALON: A legendary early Irish settler.

RONAN: A legendary king of Leinster who was deceived by his second wife into killing his first son.

TORNA: A legendary scholar.

USHEEN: The last of the Fianna.

STAGE NAMES

Names from the Great Irish Playwrights

William Butler Yeats, Sean O'Casey, and J. M. Synge were three of the greatest Irish playwrights, and all had plays that caused riots when they opened at Dublin's Abbey Theatre. Synge's most famous work, *The Playboy of the Western World*, was the last attempt to depict Irish life from the English point of view; Yeats and O'Casey, friends during the birth of Irish independence in the 1920s, were two of the first chroniclers of life as the Irish knew it.

The names from the plays of all three attest to the growing popularity of Irish names in the early part of the twentieth century:

F E M A L E

Name	Playwright	Play
ANNIE	O'Casey	*Purple Dust*
BRIDGET	Yeats	*The Land of Heart's Desire*
CATHLEEN	Yeats	*The Countess Cathleen*
	Synge	*Riders to the Sea*
DECIMA	Yeats	*The Player Queen*
DEIRDRE	Yeats	*Deirdre*
	Synge	*Deirdre of the Sorrows*
DELIA	Yeats	*Cathleen Ni Houlihan*
EEADA	O'Casey	*Red Roses for Me*
FINNOOLA	O'Casey	*Red Roses for Me*
HONOR	Synge	*The Playboy of the Western World*
JUNO	O'Casey	*Juno and the Paycock*
LAVARCHAM	Synge	*Deidre of the Sorrows*
MAISIE	O'Casey	*Juno and the Paycock*
MAURTEEN	Yeats	*The Land of Heart's Desire*
MAURYA	Synge	*Riders to the Sea*
MINNIE	O'Casey	*The Shadow of a Gunman*
MOLLY	Synge	*The Well of the Saints*
NONA	Yeats	*The Player Queen*
NORA	O'Casey	*The Plough and the Stars*
	Synge	*Riders to the Sea*
OONA	Yeats	*The Countess Cathleen*
PAUDEEN	Yeats	*The Unicorn from the Stars*
ROSIE	O'Casey	*The Plough and the Stars*

SIBBY	Yeats	*The Pot of Broth*
SOUHAUN	O'Casey	*Purple Dust*

M A L E

Name	Playwright	Play
AINNLE	Synge	*Deirdre of the Sorrows*
ALEEL	Yeats	*The Countess Cathleen*
ARDAN	Synge	*Deirdre of the Sorrows*
AYAMONN	O'Casey	*Red Roses for Me*
BARNEY	O'Casey	*The Silver Tassie*
BARTLEY	Synge	*Riders to the Sea*
BASIL	O'Casey	*Purple Dust*
CONCHUBOR	Synge	*Deirdre of the Sorrows*
CYRIL	O'Casey	*Purple Dust*
EMER	Yeats	*The Only Jealousy of Emer*
FERGIS	Synge	*Deirdre of the Sorrows*
FERGUS	Yeats	*Deirdre*
NAISI	Synge	*Deirdre of the Sorrows*
NAOISE	Yeats	*Deirdre*
OWEN	Synge	*Deirdre of the Sorrows*
PATRICK	Yeats	*Cathleen Ni Houlihan*
ROORY	O'Casey	*Red Roses for Me*
SEUMAS	O'Casey	*The Shadow of a Gunman*
SHAWN	Synge	*The Playboy of the Western World*
SHAWN	Yeats	*The Land of Heart's Desire*
SHEMUS	Yeats	*The Countess Cathleen*
SYLVESTER	O'Casey	*The Silver Tassie*
TEIGUE	Yeats	*The Countess Cathleen*

NAMES
NAMESNAMES FROM
JAMES JAMESJAMES
JOYCE JAMESJOYCE

Not so easy plucking names from the works of a writer who calls people Gush and Roaring, Mutt and Butt—reasonably straightforward in *The Dubliners,* somewhat riskier in *Ulysses,* every man for himself in *Finnegan's Wake,* but true Joyceans will recognize:

F E M A L E

ADA	KATE
ANNA LIVIA	KATHLEEN
ANNIE	KITTY
ELIZA	LILI
EVELINE	LILY
GILLIA	LISA
IRIS	MARIA
JULIA	MOLLY

MORNA   POLLY
PHILOMENA   TIZZIE

James Joyce's ABCs

There's Ada, Bett, Celia, Delia, Ena, Fretta, Gilda, Hilda, Ita, Jess, Katty, Lou (they make me cough as sure as I read them), Mina, Nippa, Opsy, Poll, Queeniee, Ruth, Saucy, Trix, Una, Vela, Wanda, Xenia, Yva, Zulma, Phoebe, Thelma. And Mee!

—Finnegan's Wake

Garden of Names

Winnie, Olive and Beatrice, Nelly and Ida, Amy and Rue. Here they come, all the gay pack, for they are the florals, from foncey and pansey to papavere's blush, foresake-me-nought, while there's leaf there's hope, with primtim's ruse and marrymay's blossom, all the flowers of the ancelles' garden.

—Finnegan's Wake

B O Y S

ALEXANDER	LEOPOLD
ANDREW	MALACHI
BANTAM	MYLES
BARNEY	NATHAN
BARTELL	NED
BLAZES	O'CONNOR
BRIAN	PATRICK/
CLIVE	PADDY/PATSY
CONOLLY	REUBEN
DENIS	ROCHE
DUNBAR	SEAN/SHAUN
FINN	SHEMUS
GABRIEL	SIMON
GARRETT	SMITH
HUGH	STEPHEN
IGNATIUS	TERENCE/TERRY
KEVIN	VALENTINE
LANTY	WISDOM
LEO	

POETIC LICENSE

Writers everywhere sometimes feel constricted by the legions of established names and feel moved to invent their own. Irish writers are no exception. The Northern Irish writer C. S. Lewis was perhaps the most inventive with names in his *Chronicles of Narnia,* which include the males Caspian, Rilian, Shasta, and Tirian. More often, however, writers concentrate their naming efforts on female characters. Here is a selection of girls' names that were the inspirations of Irish writers:

ANNA LIVIA: James Joyce drew this name from the ancient Irish name for the river Liffey: abha Lifi.

ARAVIS: An invention from C. S. Lewis's *Chronicles of Narnia.*

DAIREEN: Invented by Limerick author F. Frankfort Moore for the title character of his 1893 novel.

GLORIA: Invented by George Bernard Shaw for the 1898 play *You Never Can Tell.*

GLORVINA: Invented name for a prince's daughter in Lady Morgan's *The Wild Irish Girl,* 1806.

MALVINA: In James Macpherson's Ossianic poems, Malvina was the invented name of the lover of Oscar, grandson of Finn MacCool.

MAURYA: A character in J. M. Synge's 1904 play, *Riders to the Sea.*

ORINTHIA: George Bernard Shaw invented this name for his 1929 play *The Apple Cart.*

VEVINA: Form of Bebhinn used in Ossianic poems.

ZAIRA: Invented by the Irish writer C. R. Maturin for his novel, *Women; or, pour et contre,* 1818.

TRANSPORTERS

Sometimes particular individuals were responsible for introducing—or popularizing—their Irish monikers. The Names who carried these names include:

AIDAN	Quinn
BARRY	Fitzgerald
BRENDAN	Behan
BRIAN	Aherne
CAITLIN	(Mrs. Dylan) Thomas
CASEY	Jones
COLLEEN	Moore
DARREN	McGavin
DENNIS	Morgan
DONOVAN	(Leitch)
DUANE	Eddy
FLANN	O'Brien (b. Brian O'Nolan)
FLANNERY	O'Connor
KEELEY	Smith
KEENAN	Wynn

LIAM	O'Flaherty, Neeson
MAUREEN	O'Sullivan, O'Hara
MICKEY	Rooney, Rourke
MOIRA	Shearer
MYRNA	Loy
NOLAN	Ryan
OONA	O'Neill Chaplin
PIERCE	Brosnan
RORY	Calhoun
RYAN	O'Neal (b. Patrick)
SEAN	Connery (b. Thomas), O'Casey
	(b. John)
SHAUN	Cassidy
SINEAD	O'Connor
SIOBHAN	McKenna
TATUM	O'Neal
TYRONE	Power

Hollywood's Irish Name Problem

Evelyn Waugh describing the naming of a Hollywood starlet's new Irish persona in *The Loved One:*
  "I've spent three days trying to find a name to please her. She's turned everything down. Maureen—there are two here already; Deirdre—no one could pronounce it; Oonagh—sounds Chinese; Bridget—too common."

Not to mention:

BARNEY . . . . Google
DARRIN . . . . in "Bewitched"
DENNIS . . . . The Menace
EILEEN . . . . My Sister
FERRIS . . . . Bueller
MICKEY . . . . Mouse
MURPHY . . . . Brown
SHANE
SHERIDAN . . . . Morley
TERRY . . . . and the Pirates

THE WILD IRISH
ROSES

American popular music has, from the mid-nineteenth cen-
tury on, been a-burstin' with Irish songs. Either they waxed
nostalgic for old Erin ("It's a Long Way to Tipperary,"
"When Shall I See Ireland Again?," "Back to Donegal,"
"Christmas in Killarney"), glorified dear sainted Mother
("That Old Irish Mother of Mine," "Ireland Must Be
Heaven, For My Mother Came From There," "Mother Ma-
chree"), or celebrated the Irish in general ("When Irish Eyes
Are Smiling," "It's the Irish in Your Eye, It's the Irish in Your
Smile"). But mostly they serenaded their sweethearts, some
of whom were named:

ANNIE Rooney
Sweet ANNIE Moore
EILEEN Allanna
EILEEN Alanna
   Asthore

JENNIE, the Flower of
   Kildare
JOSEPHINE, my JO
I Wish I Could Shimmy
   Like My Sister KATE

KATHLEEN
KATHLEEN Mavour-
   neen
K-K-K-KATY
Pretty KITTY Kelly
MAGGIE Murphy's
   Home
Since MAGGIE Dooley
   Learned the Hooley
   Hooley
MARY
Tip-Top Tipperary
   MARY
Oh! What a Pal was
   MARY
MARY's a Grand Old
   Name

MOLLY O!
My Irish MOLLY O
Sweet MOLLY Malone
NELLIE Kelly, I Love
   You
PEG o' My Heart
PEGGY
PEGGY O'Neil
ROSE of Killarney
My Wild Irish ROSE
Dear Old ROSE
Sweet ROSIE O'Grady
The Daughter of ROSIE
   O'Grady
My Blushin' ROSIE

A BRIEF GUIDE TO PRONUNCIATION

The name Siobhan is a perfect illustration of many of the baffling rules of Irish pronunciation:

• S is pronounced SH before E or I: think of Sean. SH, however, is pronounced H, as is TH. In fact, the letter H, which riddles most Irish names, is particularly tricky. Read on.

• BH and MH are pronounced like a V. Or, once in a while, W.

• DH, FH, and GH are usually silent. Completely. The name Laoghaire, for instance, is pronounced Leary. Except the GH in Donoghue is pronounced like a Y. Yikes!

• CH is the only combination that makes some sense in terms of English pronunciation: it sounds like a guttural K, as in Bach.

• C and G are always hard, as in came and game.

• A is pronounced like the short O in pot; E is short as in pet, except when it comes before A, when it's silent; I is usually pronounced with a long E sound as in feed; O like the short U in put.

Accent marks, however, completely change the pronunciation of vowels: Á is pronounced *AW* as in *pawn* (or *Siobhán*), É like the long *A* in *pay*, and Ó and Ú—hallelulah!—like a long *O* (*potent*) and *OO* (*fooey*).

Then, of course, there are all the names that don't follow the usual rules. . . . If all this seems too complicated, turn the page to the indexes of girls' and boys' names, which will give you not only the proper pronunciation (in cases where there is any doubt) but also the correct Irish spelling—complete with accents, should you decide that you want to use them.

INDEX

GIRLS' NAMES

Note: Many entries in this index are followed by phoneticized spellings in parentheses, to help with pronunciation. See also A Brief Guide to Pronunciation, pages 117–118.

INDEX

BOYS' NAMES

Note: Many entries in this index are followed by phoneticized spellings in parentheses, to help with pronunciation. See also A Brief Guide to Pronunciation, pages 117–118.

Blaine, 53
Blámhac (Blavock), 78
Bláthmac (Blavock), 65
Blazes, 109
Boethius, 51
Bowes, 48
Bowie, 53
Brady, 53
Bran, 16, 48, 78, 92, 100
Brandon, 55
Brandudh (Branduff), 16, 65, 78
Branduff, 16, 65, 78
Branigan, 53
Braon (Breen), 78
Bray, 55
Brazil, 78, 84
Bréanainn (Breenan), 78, 83
Breas (Bras), 100
Breasal (Brazil), 43, 50, 65
Brecc, 78
Breccán (Brakawn), 78, 83
Brendan, xiv, 9, 20, 32, 78, 83, 86, 112
Brendanus, 32
Brennan, xiii, 53
Breslin, 53
Brian, xi, 3, 6, 8, 16, 22, 23, 27, 46, 47, 48, 60, 65, 76, 109
Bricín (Brickeen), 78
Brine (Brin), 50
Brión (Brian), 16, 100
Broderick, 53
Brody, 53
Brogan, 16, 78, 86
Brone, 16, 78
Búadach (Booak), 51
Byrne, 53

Cadhan (Kyne), 100
Cadhla (Kayla), 16
Cáel (Kale), 100
Caffar, 16, 49
Cagney, 53
Cahir, 16
Caillín (Kaleen), 65, 78
Cailte (Kilty), 100
Caimín (Commeen), 78
Cain, 44, 50
Cainneach (Konock), 27, 78
Cairbre (Karbra), 16, 78, 100
Caireall (Kerrill), 17, 78
Cairneach (Karnok), 78
Calbhach (Kalvock), 27, 48
Calhoun, 53
Callaghan, 16, 46, 50, 65, 78, 86
Callahan, 53
Calvagh, 16
Canice (Kanock), 16, 27, 78, 86
Cano, 65
Canoc, 16, 49, 51

Caoinleán (Kinlan), 18
Caolán (Kaylin), 78
Caolbhadh (Kelva), 78
Caomhán (Kevawn), 78
Carrick, 7, 55
Carroll, 16
Carthach (Karhock), 78
Carthage, 78
Cary, 55
Casey, 3, 7, 112
Cashel, 55
Cass, 78, 100
Cassair (Koseer), 78
Cassán, 78
Cassidy, 53
Cathair (Cahir), 16, 100
Cathal (Kohal), 16, 27, 65
Cathán (Kohawn), 78
Cathaoir (Kohir), 27
Cathbharr (Caffar), 49
Cavan, 55
Céadach (Kaydock), 17, 49, 51
Ceallachán (Callahan), 46, 50
Cearbhall (Carol), 27
Cearúl (Carol), 65
Ceat (Cat), 65
Cellach (Kelly), 17, 80
Celsus, 16
Cethern (Keharn), 100
Charles, xiii, 27, 29, 46, 47, 48, 49
Charlie, 11
Christian, 28
Christopher, 71, 72
Cian (Kane), 16, 17, 44, 50, 100
Cianán (Kanin), 78
Ciarán (Kieran), 17, 80, 82
Cillín (Kileen), 17, 80
Cináed (Kennay), 67
Cinnéide (Kennedy), 17
Cinnsealach (Kinsella), 17
Cionnaola (Kennelly), 17, 80, 100
Clancy, 53
Clifden, 56
Clive, 109
Cloone, 56
Clothach (Clock), 100
Cofach (Cofock), 49, 50
Coganus, 43, 49, 50
Coilín (Colin), 32
Coinneach (Konock), 16
Cole, 16
Colga, 78
Colin, 20, 32, 45
Colla, 16, 46
Colm, 16
Colmán, 16, 22, 78, 82, 86
Colmcille (Colmkilla), 16
Columba, 16, 78, 82
Columbcille (Colmkilla), 78
Comán, 78

Comhghall (Cowal), 16, 79
Comhghan (Cowan), 79
Conaire (Connery), 16, 48, 101
Conall, xiii, 16, 22, 48, 49, 65, 78, 86, 101
Conán, 16, 78, 84, 93, 101
Conchobhar (Connor), 27, 48, 65
Conchubor (Connor), 106
Congal (Connell), 65
Conlao (Conley), 78
Conley, 16, 78, 86
Conmhac (Convock), 49, 51
Conn, 16, 27, 45, 49, 50, 101
Connell, 16, 22, 53, 65
Connla, 78
Connolly, 53, 109
Connor (Conner), 9, 16, 22, 43, 48, 53, 76
Conor (Conner), 4, 9, 16, 22, 93, 101
Conroy, 53
Constantine, 27, 47
Conuil (Connell), 79
Cooey, 27
Corbally, 56
Corban, 16
Corc, 16, 50, 51, 79
Corcán, 79
Corcoran, 53, 79, 86
Cormac, 3, 16, 22, 27, 65, 79, 93, 101
Cormacán, 65
Cornelius, 27
Costello, 53
Cowal, 79
Cowan, 16, 79
Creedon, 79
Cremin, 79
Criodan (Creedon), 79
Criofan (Criffin), 17, 45, 80, 101
Críonán (Creenan), 65
Crónán, 79
Croney, 50
Cruimín (Kremin), 79
Cruinn (Krin), 65
Cú Chonnacht (Koo Kunnockt), 47
Cu Coigríche (Koo Kigrihy), 27
Cú Ula (Koo Ulla), 47, 49, 51
Cuán (Kwayne), 65, 79
Cuana (Kwayne), 66
Cuchulainn (Koo Cullen), 93, 101
Cuimín (Kimeen), 79
Cullen, 53, 56
Cullo, 47, 49, 51
Cúmhaí (Koovy), 18, 27, 45, 46, 47, 49, 50
Cumhal (Kooval), 101
Cúmheá (Koovey), 47